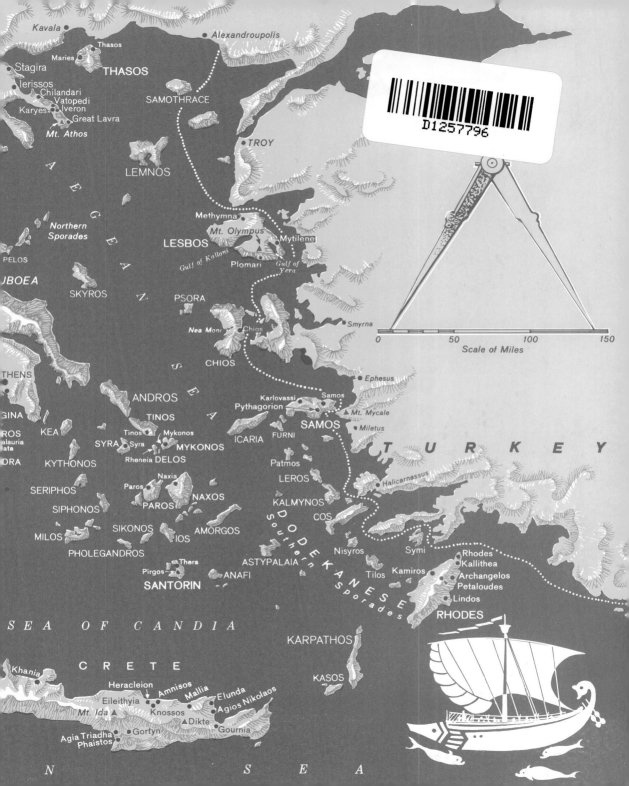

Kavala

Thasos
Maries
THASOS

Stagira
Ierissos
Chilandari
Vatopedi
Karyes
Iveron
Great Lavra
Mt. Athos

Alexandroupolis

SAMOTHRACE

TROY

LEMNOS

A E G E A N

Northern Sporades

PELOS

Methymna
Mt. Olympus
Mytilene
LESBOS
Gulf of Kalloni
Plomari
Gulf of Yera

Smyrna

JBOEA

SKYROS

PSORA

Nea Moni Chios
CHIOS

S E A

THENS

ANDROS

Ephesus

Karlovassi
Samos
Pythagorion
Mt. Mycale
SAMOS
Miletus

TINOS

GINA

ROS
alauria
lata
DRA

KEA

Tinos
SYRA Syra
Rheneia

Mykonos
MYKONOS
DELOS

ICARIA
FURNI

T U R K E Y

KYTHONOS

Patmos

LEROS

Halicarnassus

SERIPHOS

Naxia
Paros
PAROS
NAXOS

SIPHONOS

MILOS

SIKONOS
IOS
AMORGOS

PHOLEGANDROS

Thera
Pirgos
SANTORIN

ANAFI

ASTYPALAIA

KALMYNOS

COS

D O D E K A N E S E
Southern Sporades

Nisyros

Tilos

Symi

Kamiros

Rhodes
Kallithea
Archangelos
Petaloudes
Lindos

RHODES

S E A   O F   C A N D I A

KARPATHOS

KASOS

C R E T E

Khania

Heracleion
Eileithyia
Amnisos
Mallia
Elunda
Agios Nikolaos
Mt. Ida
Knossos
Dikte
Gournia
Agia Triadha
Gortyn
Phaistos

N

S E A

Scale of Miles
0   50   100   150

ROBERT PAYNE

The Isles of Greece

WITH PHOTOGRAPHS BY

ALEXANDER ARTEMAKIS

SIMON AND SCHUSTER • NEW YORK

for
CHRISTOS DAMIGOS
who chose to be born during
our wanderings

Contents

Now Crete remains, and Salamis is green
In the darkening shade of her laurel leaves,
While Delos, crowned with a wreath of fiery rays,
Lifts her head, drunk with thought, to the sunrise,
And there are enough purple fruit on Tinos for
                    everyone,
And in Chios too there is ripe fruit; the Cyprian
                    liquor
Flows from the drunken hills; and from Calauria
The silver streams slip down to the sea
To the ancient waters of the Father.
All are living still, the islands, mothers of heroes,
Flowering from year to year . . .

          —Friedrich Hölderlin, "The Archipelagus"

Invitation to a Voyage

THE TRAVELER coming to the Greek islands for the first time must be prepared for miracles. He will see colors he has never seen before, skies he has never dreamed of, and he will dwell in an air which is wholly transparent and crystal pure. He will see islands like swans, peacocks and tigers, islands the color of flame and islands the color of bone. He will see inaccessible golden-columned temples perched on the sheer edges of cliffs, and he will climb to them as easily as he takes an afternoon walk. He will see the gods and heroes walking in the sky, stepping lightly over mountains, and he will find himself remembering the details of battles in which he fought thousands of years ago. Time will vanish; on lonely beaches and in sunlit bays he will enter timelessness. In the evenings he will see the islands vanishing, only to be transformed into sleeping maidens and moonlit lions, and in the dead of night he will hear the ancient ceremonies. The Phoenix's nest is not in Arabia, but in the seas of Greece where everything is born again, out of sea-spray and the shining air.

To sail in a caïque from one island to another is to know a pleasure which is never sated by enjoyment, to become emperor of all one surveys. One can go quietly mad among the islands, and never recover. Islomania is a disease with no known cure, attacking young and old alike, and those who suffer from it can be recognized by the faraway look in their eyes, their horror of enclosed spaces, and their lust for certain colors, such as royal blue with depths upon depths of gold in it, which can only be seen in the Aegean and along the coasts of Greece, though sometimes a pale reflection of them appears in Byzantine mosaics. Islomania is a dread disease. Men have left their wives and children in order to wander from one island to another, and some have never returned.

I know a Dutch sea captain who loves islands so much that when he sails his liner from New York to Rotterdam he must skirt the Scillies off the west coast of England and imperil his ship simply for the pleasure of looking at those islands which are mere rusted teeth compared with the islands of the East Indies where he had sailed in his youth. If you ask him why he puts a thousand people in jeopardy every time he crosses the Atlantic, he answers simply: "What else is so beautiful as islands?" The Dutch are among the worst sufferers of islomania, for they remember the seas of Java and the Celebes dotted with islands green with palms and pepper trees, but the English run them close. They have the islands off Malaya to dream about, and the West Indies where they fitted out their privateers. The English, being islanders themselves, suffer from a particularly morbid and virulent form of the disease and long ago abandoned a search for a cure.

The Greeks have cured themselves of islomania by a long process of withdrawal and disintoxication. I have known men born in the islands who settled in Athens and never returned for fear of the enchantment which the islands wield over them. "I come from Samos, or from Thera, or from Lesbos," they will say, and when you ask them when they last saw their birthplace they will talk about Dow-Jones averages and shipping rates and the latest scandal in the Athenian court. They will go to any lengths to avoid talking about the islands where their poverty-stricken grandparents remain. On the whole, the islands are poor and desolate places, without the creature comforts of Athens. For them to return to the islands is to be committed to provincial isolation, where there is no jazz hot and people still live according to their ancient ways. Also, they are afraid of the spell which the islands cast on them.

Spells and visions accompany the traveler in the Greek islands. He will have the illusion that the islands are living presences, not lumps of rock jutting up through the sea. They are not anchored, but float across the water, and seem always to be coming toward you. You have the illusion that the air has dropped away, and some thinner and rarer substance has been substituted. Here light becomes power, fierce and unrelenting, and the air becomes crystal fire. The reds are a deeper red and the blues are a deeper blue in the heart of the Phoenix's nest.

The quality of the light shining over Greece is of a transparent purity unknown elsewhere. Go to the islands, and you will see purity refined until it becomes something else altogether. Here light becomes edible, and eyes become mouths. It is a light that can be drunk and tasted, full of ripeness, filtering through flesh and marble, almost palpable. It fumes and glares, and has a life of its own. It is in perpetual movement, flashing off the wave-caps, flashing off the sea onto the rocks, flashing from one mountain peak to another and back again, never still. This light shouts and exults, and seems to be conscious of its exuberant powers. Flowing like spring water, it fills all the heavens. There is no rest from it. It is pitiless and demanding, searching out every cranny. No wonder the ancient Greeks thought of the light as divine, with the earth and sea as its thrones. They gave it the physical presence of a god and called it Phoebus Apollo, the god of the divine radiance, and they characteristically chose for his birthplace the small bare rocky island of Delos set in the peacock-blue seas of the Aegean.

When you come to the Greek islands, you leave one world to enter another where nothing is what it seems to be. That small bent man climbing the hill on his mule is Odysseus returning to Penelope in disguise; he has not changed over the centuries; it is the same Odysseus. That sailor, who has spent the morning cleaning his nets and now in the afternoon puts to sea, is Agamemnon setting sail for Troy; when he returns there will be a purple carpet waiting for him, and he will die in the arms of Clytemnestra. The legends live on, remaining alive because the light summons them. In the visionary landscape of the islands one sees the gods walking every day, the heroes beside them. They live by virtue of that imperious light welling from the earth, the sea and the sky, making everything larger than life. "The gods are present in the sky." This is the first article of faith learned by the sufferer from islomania, and by the intensity of his belief you can gauge whether he can ever be cured of his disease.

We speak of the clarity of the island air, but it is not a continuous clarity. It comes and goes with the pulses of the sun. The purest light comes with the dawn, and for the rest of the morning purity parades in ornate, jewel-like garments. Then about noon a heat haze spills over the sea and the hills, and descends like a curtain from the sky, and the transparent light withdraws a little. In the afternoon the pure light returns, more jubilant than ever, marching across the earth with an almost human grandeur, proud of its brilliance and its solemn march. The Greeks tend to sleep during the haze of noon, and therefore rarely see the light clouded. When darkness falls, they hurry to light as many lamps as possible, for they are afraid of the dark.

The islanders, who live in this light and never see any other, are therefore the most enviable of people. They are all princes living out their lives in palaces, with jeweled colors permanently in attendance. They live simply on bread, fish, olives, pulse and wine, and few are wealthy, yet they walk with dignity, as though they were perfectly aware that nature was determined to please them. The islanders of Santorin, living on the top of their flame-colored cliffs in snow-white houses, may be the most favored of all people, for wherever they look they see beauty which to others is breathtaking, but which they regard as commonplace. So, too, in the northern island of Thasos, where the streets are of marble, you come across a small fishing village occupying only a small part of an ancient town, consisting of four or five streets and a hundred rose gardens; and the ancient ruins are so much a part of the village that the inhabitants for at least half their lives must be living in ancient Greece. Or go to Lindos, with its streets of black and white pebbles lying at the foot of a honey-colored acropolis, with the temple of Athena standing on the cliff-edge, with columns and colonnades and stairways still in place, all rose-red against the royal blue of the sea and the yellow sands, and you find yourself wondering whether there is any other place on earth where light falls so majestically on a scene so majestically created. It is as though the rivers of heaven had washed the light clean, and created a new kind of light altogether in which everything seems to be pure, perfect and eternal.

On the acropolis at Lindos, at noon, when the tourists have departed and the old gate-keeper has fallen asleep and the village lies silent below, the golden rock, the rose-red columns and the blue sea can take possession of you so strongly that you are in danger of losing your mind, in danger of becoming one of those who, like the poet Friedrich Hölderlin, was so entranced by ancient Greece that he slipped out of the present world altogether and spent the last forty years of his life in a visionary world of his own making.

No one ever wrote so well of the Greek islands as Hölderlin, who never saw them, but dreamed of them throughout his waking life. His poem "The Archipelagus" is a hymn in praise of the divine fire glowing over the islands. In one of his last poems, written on the edge of madness, he wrote: *"O Insel des Lichts!"* O island of light! and this was enough to set him lamenting for the lost glory. In another poem he wrote:

> *O land of Homer!*
> *By the scarlet cherry tree, or when*
> *Sent by you in the vineyard I see*
> *The young peaches hanging green,*
> *And the swallow comes from afar, telling tales*
> *While building his house on my walls,*
> *Then, O Ionia, I dream of you*
> *In the days of May under the stars.*
> *Therefore I have come, O islands, to see you . . .*

So one goes to the Greek islands for the sake of the light welling in those visionary heavens, and this is enough reason for going. The strange radiance in the air, the gold in the sky shining like heavenly swords, all those veils of crystal which fall one by one to reveal a landscape which itself seems to be formed of crystal, all these beckon the traveler and demand his devotion. It was a Greek who first called Christ "the light of lights," thereby showing first that he was Greek and second that he believed that light was holy. The light over the Greek islands is a light to live by.

But it is not only for the sake of the light that one goes to the islands. The origins of western civilization are rooted in the islands. In Crete, Samos and Delos especially we see the first deliberate steps which led by devious ways toward our dangerous preoccupation with freedom, with technology, and with man's steady conquest over nature. From Delos Apollo blessed lucidity of mind, becoming the protector of the human reason. The youthful god with the silver bow presided over the clear intelligence and waged war against the ancient power of myths. He proclaimed the existence of order against the fierce disorders of mythology, and became the champion of the arts and sciences. No one knows where he came from. The Greeks believed that he vanished during the winter in the far distant north, returning to Greece with the spring swallows. He was a mysterious god, so youthful, so beautiful and debonair, with so many contraries mixed up in him, that he is almost beyond conceiving. He cured and he killed. He fostered the arts of medicine and he hurled the plague at his enemies, and was as vengeful as Athena. Everywhere you go in the Greek islands you will see the temples erected to him, and in Naxos you will see a solitary gateway of creamy marble which remains as an invitation to a voyage among his islands, for even now he seems to rule over them. The god of the divine radiance uses the islands as his stepping-stones.

Yet it was in Samos, under the protection of the goddess Hera, that engineering achieved its first remarkable results. These feats so dazzled Herodotus that he found himself compelled to describe them at length, and though he had seen them with his own eyes, he found difficulty in believing them. There, during the reign of the tyrant Polycrates, the engineer Eupalinos constructed a tunnel through a mountain to bring water to the capital, boring from both ends. It was the first aqueduct carved through a mountain, and could have been conceived only by a strictly mathematical mind. The other two feats depended less on mathematics than on an unremitting sense of organization. The temple of Hera, built on the seashore, was the largest known up to that time, and from its size and its colonnades with triple rows of columns was known as "the Labyrinth." The deep-water harbor, also built at the orders of Polycrates, was an engineering feat of comparable magnitude. From Samos, too, came the great innovators Aristarchus and Pythagoras, whose researches were of crucial importance in the history of human ideas, for they set astronomy and mathematics on the paths they still follow. If Samos had produced only Pythagoras, it would have been enough.

Samos, then, gave to the western mind the impulse to inquire and to construct according to scientific law. The gifts of Crete are not so easily defined, for they belong more to the realm of aesthetics and to the mind's adventures among shapes and colors. A Minoan vase painted with flowers or fish or the swirling tentacles of an octopus has a freedom and a feeling for life which shames our own efforts to be free in paint. They painted without recourse to dogma. They looked at life with wide-open eyes, while the artists of Sumeria and

Egypt saw life through veils of tradition and shadows of dread. No doubt the rule of the Minoan kings was tyrannical, but the artists painted with an exquisite tenderness and affection for the things they loved and desired to see perpetuated. Their strenuous and free-flowing paintings are also a part of our freedom.

There is still one other reason for visiting the islands. The uncreated light pours from the heavens on the islands where the western mind first came to maturity, but it is not enough to enjoy the holy light and to go on pilgrimage to the places where the modern world was born. The beauty of the islands is reason enough for going, for all are sculptured in a different way. Geologically they may be of the same stock as the mainland, children long severed from the mother but retaining her characteristic features. Yet this is not the impression they give when you sail among them. Thickly wooded Lesbos, drowned in olive trees, might be a thousand miles away from neighboring Chios with its gaunt golden-sided mountains barren of ornament. Santorin, scorched by ancient volcanic flames, rising vertically a thousand feet in the air, has nothing in common with the swan-like island of Delos which lies so close to the water that it is in danger of being carried away in the sea's flood. While Tinos has a certain faint resemblance to Myconos, Rhodes and Crete could be on different continents. Each island is a world of its own, with its own customs, colors and shapes, and its own separate history. They are like many-colored jewels scattered over a blue ground, here a diamond, there a sapphire, a ruby, or an emerald. Sailing among the islands you find yourself in a jewel-encrusted sea.

The Greeks believed passionately in the Islands of the Blessed, where the souls of the fortunate ones travel after death, but since

none had ever returned from the dead to describe the blessed islands, they imagined that their souls journeyed among islands very
like their own. Plutarch tells the story of the boy Timarchus who
fell into despair when his friend, who happened to be the son of
Socrates, died; and so he went down to the cave of Trophonius in
the hope of dying there and meeting his friend. As he related his
experiences later, he found himself in a great darkness and was
afterward transported into a region of pure transparent air filled
with sweet voices. There was no land in sight, only innumerable
islands where men dwelt in a blue ocean, and these islands seemed
to be bathed in fire and were continually changing color "as though
they were being painted," and what was most extraordinary about
the islands was that some were moving and others standing still,
and some seemed to be sinking below the surface of the sea. He was
not quite sure whether it was a sea or a vast lake, but he was sure he
had seen the islands turning all the colors of the rainbow, and
sometimes they would assume murky colors "like those in
marshes." Only a very few of the islands moved in a straight course,
for the majority moved according to a kind of spiraling orbit, never
coming back to the same point.

Timarchus went on to describe his adventures as he traveled
among the islands in the sea of heaven, seeing everything clearly
and noting the places where the sea was shallow and where it was
fathoms deep. He seemed at once to be looking down at the sea
from a high place, and to be sailing among the painted islands. He
saw places where the blue sea turned mysteriously white and other
places where chasms opened and there came the voices of lamenting children, but always there was the spectacle of the wheeling
islands perpetually changing color, and nearly always they were
beautiful.

For a long time he gazed at the islands, and then he heard a voice saying: "Timarchus, what do you wish to learn?"

"Everything," Timarchus replied, "for everything is wonderful."

So it is with the modern traveler among the Greek islands, where everything is wonderful. In his own lifetime, without troubling to die, he can sail among the Islands of the Blessed.

Rhodes

ON EVERY DAY of the year the port of Piraeus is alive with ships. The great liners come sailing in, painted in immaculate colors, but they have the appearance of strangers entering the port on sufferance. The real owners are the crowds of island steamers, squat ugly ships, noisy and not very comfortable, having the look of old bedraggled hens which have lost most of their feathers. They chug along from one island to another with an assurance which the captains of liners might envy. They know all the roads of the sea, and they are the true descendants of the ancient penteconters which once ruled the Aegean.

Go to a travel agent in Athens and ask him how to reach the island of Samos, and he will spend half an hour on the telephone and finally he will give you a ticket for a purely mythical ship going to the wrong island. In Piraeus there will be a signboard outside the ship telling you where it is going. You have only to walk on the ship to know that you will reach the island, although if the signboard says it is leaving at six o'clock, it must be understood that there is no question of mathematical accuracy. Ships leave when they want to leave. Among the Greek islands the captain is the lord of time.

We learned these things the hard way, for we traveled as we pleased, taking whatever means of transportation was available. We traveled by foot, by truck, by bus, on mules and donkeys, in airplanes, in little thirty-foot caïques, and for a brief period on a luxury cruise ship which resembled a newly baked cake laced with icing. We sailed from Samos to Lesbos on a rusted tramp steamer loaded down to the gunwales with drums of olive oil, and most of the drums were leaking. We flew from Lesbos to Athens in a two-engine plane which was remarkable only because the stewardess went white at take-off and spent the rest of the flight saying her prayers with a fervor which caused us to wonder whether we should imitate her. We sailed to Poros, Hydra and Spetsai on a hydrofoil which skimmed the water at thirty-three miles an hour. In the end we realized that it might have been simpler if we had always taken the island steamers and jumped ship whenever we pleased.

Some of the island steamers are forty years old; they grunt and squeak and rumble; there are rumors that when they are breaking apart, they are cannibalized. I suspect that the island steamers we traveled on were cannibalized, made up of the little steamers which cross the Norwegian fjords with some admixture from the Merseyside paddle-wheelers. They were well protected with an assortment of holy icons; there were never less than ten icons to a ship. The saints protected them. You had the feeling that the captain knew the islands so well that he would lead you to them even if he were blindfolded. Assurance rested lightly on his shoulders, for he would steer the ship into port and five minutes later he would be backing out again. In the interval he had disembarked his passengers, their luggage and their crates of chickens, and he had stowed into the holds several tons of marble.

S.S. EPIRUS   *Friday 6 P.M.*
Syra—Tinos—Myconos—Karlovasi—Samos

S.S. AIGEUS   *Sunday 12 P.M.*
Patras—Ithaca—Acarnania—Leucadia—Corcyra—Brindisi

S.S. MAULENA   *Wednesday 7 P.M.*
Kea—Cythnos—Seriphos—Siphnos—Melos—Syra

Such were the signboards which stood on the dock at Piraeus. Would you go to Ithaca and see the homeland of Odysseus, or to Melos and search for the missing arms of Aphrodite? There is no need to mount a vast expedition. You simply walk up the gang-plank and wait for someone to sell you a ticket. You can buy beer and brandy and sandwiches on board, and at six o'clock, or in God's good time, you will sail for the islands. One can get drunk in Piraeus simply by looking at these signboards.

The island steamers smell of mahogany and diesel oil, and have few comforts. The little bar will have precious few of the things you want, the lavatory will be choked, and the officers will be unshaved and down at heel. At night especially, when the electric lights are dimmed, the steamers take on a strangely Victorian look, so that you wonder whether you have not entered another century. But these are minor discouragements. Travel on a luxury cruise ship and you will receive impeccable service; there will be films and dances on alternate nights; there will be prizes for the woman wearing the funniest hat and for the man wearing the funniest mustache; and the entertainment counselor will drive you out of your mind. The island steamer is earthier. There will be shouts and songs and dances, and beer will spill over the lounge. The Greeks know how to travel. They spread out a blanket, set the whole family on it, and then engage in the national sport they have pursued for three thousand years, gambling with drachmas, buttons, breadcrumbs or matchsticks; and when they weary of gambling, they suddenly jump up and dance, not touching one another, but each one grasping a handkerchief held in another's hand, and in this way they form a ring of acrobatic dancers; and there are few things more pleasant than to watch them dancing and singing their mournful songs as the sun goes down over the islands.

Night in the Aegean is thick with ghosts: so they sprawl about on deck in each other's arms, and that too is something which is forbidden on the cruise ships. During the long nights the island steamers slacken pace for safety's sake, and the ships travel at a walking pace. White rocks loom out of the darkness, a Venetian fortress appears high up on a crag, lights glow and then die out on distant islands. Sometimes, if you are lucky, you will see the ancient penteconters racing through the sea-mist.

The Temple of Athena Lindia

If I could have my way, I would travel straight from Piraeus to Lindos, but few ships any longer enter that forgotten port where St. Paul once came to bring the gospel to the Lindians. I would arrive at dawn and anchor half a mile offshore to watch the sun rising over Asia Minor and pouring its light on that great golden cliff crowned with the temple of Athena Lindia. In all of Greece there is no more lovely temple than this.

Sometimes, it is true, a private yacht will anchor off Lindos, but the island steamers come not at all, and the best you can hope for is a tramp steamer. It is simpler to cross the island from Rhodes, which can be reached from Athens by air. It is a good road, winding close to the sea, a road which seems to have been constructed to show the island at its best advantage. The hills soar, have sharp edges, and remind you of the mainland of Greece. Elsewhere on the island the hills are softer and more oriental. Yet the island of Rhodes belongs to the Orient, and Lindos faces Egypt.

Along that road flows the smell of the wild thyme from the hills and the sea wind, and here and there the sweeter smell of orchards. Small white villages appear, the houses like cubes of glittering salt. Aphandou, which means "invisible," appears only to disappear, nestling in the low hills. Archangelos lies in a broad valley and is seen first from the brow of a hill like a vast white checkerboard lying below, all the squares fitting neatly together, with many shades of white and silver. The exhilarating road winds beneath the sun-bleached mountains and over rivers which are no more than a trickle among stones. Here, for most of the year, the sun is pitiless.

But although there are few roads on the Greek islands to compare with this, nothing prepares you for the spectacle of the acropolis at Lindos. Suddenly the road mounts, clinging to a shelf of rock, and just as suddenly it dips into a valley. There before you, gold in the sun, lies the great headland with the beetling cliffs. Faintly in the distance, like lace, stand the ancient walls and the rose-red columns.

> *On the summit of the citadel of Lindos, thou art*
> *O Athena, the glory of this ancient city . . .*

Those words can be found in the Greek Anthology, but they only hint at the perfection of the scene. Imagine the Acropolis at Athens set on the edge of a cliff overlooking a sea of the most intense royal blue flecked with gold; imagine that instead of the rubble at the foot of the Parthenon there are orderly rows of columns, arcades and colonnades, and a wide stairway leading to the temple; imagine an air of the purest blue, fountains of blue air leaping up the side of the cliff and forming a kind of sunlit archway high above the temple area; and then imagine that for good measure there has been added in one corner of the headland a castle of the Knights of St. John and a ruined Byzantine church so placed that they do not interrupt the view over the temple of Athena Lindia, but form a gateway to it, reinforcing the dignity of the goddess, making her all the more beautiful by association with shapes and forms foreign to her. This cliff is her dwelling place, and no one knows for how many centuries she has lived there.

We do not know how she came to birth, or what heroic feats she performed on behalf of her people. Her legends are unknown. We know that when the island of Rhodes was in danger from the Persians and from Demetrius Poliorcetes, she appeared mysteriously to the Lindians and led them to victory in much the same way that Theseus led the Athenians to victory at Marathon. Like the Athena who ruled over Athens, she was a warlike goddess, merciless to her enemies, proud and invincible. She does not appear on the coins of Lindos, which have a dolphin on one side and a roaring lion on the other. In her small temple on the cliff-edge she was represented by an image carved out of wood and ivory. The image was lifesize, for the temple on the cliff-edge was too small to permit a vast monumental figure.

Although no portrait of her has survived, and her history is unknown, we know almost as much about her as we want to know, for the shape of the temple on the cliff must be an abstract portrait of her. It appears that she was born in the sacred cave scooped out of the cliff-face immediately below her temple; the cave is now sacred to the Virgin. Half-bird, half-goddess, she belonged to the high places, and was venerated for her power to still the tempests. The Lindians were always sailors and adventurers, and she was their protectress, accompanying them on their pirate raids and their journeys across the seas. The Lindians founded Gela in Sicily, and Thucydides tells us that the acropolis and fortress of Gela was named after her.

Long before the city of Rhodes came into being, Lindos was powerful, trading with Egypt and Phoenicia, her long slender ships famous for their speed. Under Cleobulos, tyrant of Lindos in the sixth century, the power of Lindos reached its greatest extent, and Cleobulos himself became one of the Seven Sages of Greece, chiefly famous because he was the first to announce the words which pleased Apollo so much that they were engraved in the forecourt of his temple at Delphi: "Nothing in excess." On a bare rock below the cliff lies the empty tomb of the sage, of whom we know only that he traveled in Egypt, wrote thousands of verses and was reputed to be very beautiful. In those parts of southern France settled by the Rhodians the name of Cléobule can still be heard.

Herodotus tells us that among the gifts offered to Athena Lindia by King Amasis of Egypt was a linen gown embroidered with gold thread and with a number of animal figures woven into it, and the most remarkable thing about the gown was that each thread consisted of three hundred and sixty strands. In 1904 the Danish archeologists discovered the chronicle of the temple of Athena Lindia; it had been turned face downward and was used as the pavement of an early Christian church on the west slope of the acropolis. The gifts to the goddess were listed. They included the gown presented by King Amasis, and various treasures offered by King Minos of Crete, by King Artaphernes of Persia, by Alexander the Great, and many others. Menelaus and Helen had both visited the shrine of the goddess. Helen had left a cup shaped like her own breast.

The Danish archeologists were able to reconstruct the history of the temple. It had been burned and rebuilt several times, being completed in its present form only in 208 B.C. Pindar speaks of the many statues in the porticoes, and they found the pedestals and set them up again. Below the great terrace where the temple stands, a long row of bronze statues once stood, and you can still see the clamps which once riveted them to the marble pedestals and the long inscriptions testifying to the achievements of the heroes who were permitted to stand guard over the shrine.

The cliff of Lindos is a sculptured work, beautiful in itself, red and green and russet layers of rock breaking the uneven surface. From the temple there is a sheer drop of four hundred feet to the sea. The sacred cave just below the temple is only one of many caves honeycombing the cliff; if you take a boat and sail round the cliff, you can make your way into four or five caves each the size of a house, glowing mysteriously, quiet except for the crying of the gulls who build their nests among the stalagmites.

To come to Lindos on a summer day, to bathe by the sandy half-moon beach, and then to wander slowly through the white streets past houses which still preserve their intricately carved Byzantine façades, and then at noon to climb to the summit of the acropolis is to know a pleasure which never changes. Noon is best, for this is the time when the old guardian locks the gates and goes to sleep. Slip past him, and all the temple is yours.

This high and holy temple on the cliffs is a perilous place. It can wrench the heart and make you want to stay in Lindos forever, or at least to return every year. It is a good place to begin a journey to the islands, for everything you see later will have to be measured against the towering beauty of Athena Lindia.

The Painter

He was a small dark man with bushy hair, black-rimmed spectacles, and the look of a young student. He smiled easily, and moved like a cat, with the authority of a cat. He wore an open-neck shirt, a black pullover and black trousers, and there was a certain elegance about him, and a certain distance. His name was Savva Giakoumakis. He was a potter and a painter, and he could be found nearly every day of the year in a small shack at the thirty-first kilometer from Rhodes on the road to Lindos.

He paints inside the shack. Outside he has his potter's wheel and banks of clay, some geranium-red, others bluish-grey, all moist and ready for the wheel. In less than five minutes he will shape a clay vase of impeccable delicacy on his wheel, and in less than twenty seconds he will paint a running deer on a black fired plate. We watched him and timed him. He composed the deer in twelve swift strokes, and no doubt he had painted ten thousand deer in his time and would go on to paint ten thousand more, but this deer lived and breathed. Familiarity had not dulled his eye or hand. With two strokes he painted the deer's horns, with another swift curving stroke he painted the back and hindquarters, four flecks of white paint produced the running hooves. It was not dexterity only, but knowledge, patient study, a perfect sense of proportion. He went about the task like a man who could have done it blindfolded.

The painters and potters of Rhodes were renowned in classical times and again in the Middle Ages. Rhodian ware was deeply prized by the Romans, and in the seventeenth century there were schools of magnificent pottery makers on the island. The exuberance and the rich colors derive from ancient Greece, but the feeling is always new. They liked to paint ships with crowded sails, but these ships are curiously empty of emotion, cumbrous and stilted, rarely successful. The best are the young animals and the sprays of flowers, deer, young calves, sheaks of poppies, garlands of golden lupines and lilies. No doubt they painted the ship so often because the great Carrack of the Knights of St. John with its eight decks and hundreds of cannon was one of the wonders of the world, to be remembered through all the generations of Turkish rule. They flaunted it, and then grew weary of it. But from the beginning, ever since Apollo took possession of the island, Rhodes gloried in its flowers. The ancient coins of Rhodes were stamped with the image of a rose.

There are pottery shops all over Rhodes and they clutter the narrow streets of Lindos. About one-tenth of the painted plates are magnificent. Why it should happen that nine-tenths should be disastrous is something of a mystery, for the standard of the best is amazingly high. For four or five dollars you can obtain a plate which is a masterpiece of color and design, and there is no better bargain to be found anywhere in Greece.

The Lion of Venice

The lion sits quietly in the courtyard of the museum at Rhodes, mottled with age, heavy-chested, his paws flung out in front of him. Time has made sockets of his eyes, but he is imperious still with his face of marble enclosed in a flowing mane.

You find him all over the Greek islands, for the Venetians left indelible traces of their presence. They were traders, fortress builders, Crusaders, captains of merchantmen, sackers of cities. The lion of St. Mark prowled the eastern Mediterranean; for nearly three hundred years he was the most powerful force in the islands. The

Athenians came to power by conquering the islands; so, too, did the Venetians. The islands were their trade marts, their naval bases, their stepping stones.

Yet this lion sitting in the courtyard at Rhodes is not what he seems to be. He is indisputably Venetian, but he has almost no business being here. Rhodes is one of the few islands which the Venetians held only briefly. In 1082 A.D. they received commercial privileges in Rhodes from the Byzantine emperor, but within a hundred and fifty years the Genoese were in possession. Then came the Knights of St. John, refugees from Jerusalem and Cyprus, who held the island until it was conquered by Suleyman the Magnificent in 1522 A.D. The lion, then, must belong to the early years of the Venetian settlement, long before the Knights of St. John built their fortified palaces. He sits among the ancient tombs, the cannonballs, and the altars wreathed with ox-skulls as though he had been there from the beginning of time.

When Suleyman the Magnificent brought up his heavy siege engines and invested the island with a force of about two hundred thousand men, only a pitiably small army opposed him. There were six hundred and fifty Knights, and they were assisted by some two hundred Genoese seamen, fifty Venetians, four hundred Canadians, and perhaps six thousand native Rhodians. The siege lasted for six months, the Turks blockading the town from the sea and seizing the high points of the island, where they installed their siege-guns. A Spanish Knight turned traitor, and the Knights were finally forced to surrender. The survivors were not massacred, but permitted to leave in good order. They sailed for Malta, exchanging the most luxuriant of the Mediterranean islands for the most barren.

The visitor to Rhodes may be excused if he finds himself wondering how the Turks could have remained in possession for nearly four hundred years and left so few traces. There are four or five mosques, a Turkish cemetery, some blue-tiled fountains; a handful of Turkish farmers cultivate their fields; on the whole island there cannot be more than three or four hundred of them, and the dead outnumber the living. Though the Knights of St. John sailed from the island long ago, they are still vividly present. Their huge fortress walls, palaces and archways remain. The Italians during their brief tenure—they captured the island from the Turks in 1912 and lost it in World War II—helped to restore the great buildings which became romantic ruins under the Turks, and though they restored the Grand Master's palace too well, they were splendidly accurate in their reconstruction of the ancient walls.

From the sea the battlemented walls shine like dusky gold, pretty as toys. Windmills revolve along the mole, their transparent sails catching the light and throwing pale dappled shadows on the walls. There are only three or four windmills, but they have the effect of a forest of welcoming arms. The sea is the deep crystalline blue of ripening grapes held up to the sun. As far as the eye can see, there are only mediaeval castle walls, fortresses and battlements.

To enter the harbor at Rhodes on a clear summer morning is to see the grandeur of the Middle Ages at a single glance. Aigues-Mortes and Carcassonne, which are also surrounded with mediaeval walls, merely suggest the Middle Ages; their walls do not have that savage, uncompromising power. The walls of Rhodes speak of the desire of mediaeval man to protect himself to the uttermost: only by treachery could the enemy enter. Twice there were major sieges. The Sultan of Egypt laid siege to the city in 1444, and was repulsed. Again in 1480 the Turks under Mehemet II laid siege to the city, bringing up a huge fleet of 160 ships. The Knights under the Grand Master Pierre d'Aubusson held out from the end of May until the beginning of August when in despair the Turks lifted the siege. "In all the world I never saw a place so well defended," wrote Merri Dupui, a French traveler who visited Rhodes shortly after the siege, and so it was. Rhodes was unconquerable except from within. The walls that seem like toys from the sea are sometimes forty feet thick.

The Turks saw no reason to dismantle the walls, or even to improve on them. Old drawings and miniatures, and some photographs taken in the last century, show that they regarded the city of the Knights with a kind of protective indifference. If a wall fell, they made no effort to put it up again, and they changed nothing. In the long steep Street of the Knights which leads to the Grand Master's palace, the armorial bearings still stand above the doorways, and it seems never to have occurred to the Turks to remove them. So again they changed nothing in the superb Gothic hospital of the Knights where, according to a contemporary traveler, the sick lay in curtained beds and were served meat on silver plates and wine in silver cups.

In Rhodes the power of the Knights is so extensive that it overshadows not only the Turks, but the ancient Greeks. In a small corner of the hospital there is a museum, chiefly notable for a marble Venus dredged from the sea, beautiful still, though the sea has pounded her into a shape she never possessed. She stands in a corner, serene yet inconsolable, surrounded by Hellenistic statues which have none of her authority. Armless, almost faceless, the remnant of a remnant, her head broken at the neck, her torn skirts clinging to her knees, she still has power to take the breath away, for her young body still sings.

Outside in the courtyard, under an archway, the lion of Venice waits impassively. He listens indifferently to the call of the muezzin and the tolling of the church bells; he has seen the Knights come and go, and the Turks, and the British who briefly occupied the island. He was there at the beginning, and he seems to have no regrets.

Crete

THE EMBLEM of Rhodes was the rose; the emblem of Crete was the labyrinth. The one was open to the sun, gentle and beautiful; the other was dark, contrived, mysterious and sinister.

We see the rose and the labyrinth on the ancient coins, but the coins are deceptive. Outwardly Crete shows no signs of being sinister. The mountains have an austere beauty, the land is wonderfully fertile with sixteen feet of topsoil and inexhaustible layers of fresh water lying below. Ash and cypress grow along the banks of the streams; the vines grow shoulder-high; the thickset olive trees stretch for miles. Compared with the gaunt valleys of Greece, Crete is paradise. No wonder the ancient Greeks looked with longing at Crete and invested the island with mystery and enchantment.

The mystery remains—the mystery of an ancient empire which vanished overnight in flame and flood, leaving the ruins of cities and palaces decorated with bright frescoes. For more than sixty years archaeologists have been excavating their cities, and with every excavation we seem to be further away from an understanding of these people. Who was Minos? What was the labyrinth? Where are the graves of the kings who ruled so despotically and for so long? Since they were seamen and pirates, where were their ports and shipyards? What was the significance of the double-headed ax, and how much truth is there in the legend of Theseus and Ariadne? Sometimes the mystery lifts for a moment; then the darkness comes down again.

You step off the ship at Heracleion and within two minutes you can be in the museum which contains the largest collection of Minoan treasures in the world; within twenty minutes you can reach Knossos. Not far from Heracleion is Mallia, a small Minoan city on the seacoast. Half a day's journey to the east is Gournia, another city riding down a hillside and overlooking the sea, with a spectacular view over the dark and wrinkled mountains of the bay of Mirabello; but neither Mallia nor Gournia suggests the power of an invincible empire, and Knossos itself gives the impression of having been a ceremonial capital or a summer palace. Only at Phaistos on the southern coast is there the sense of unbridled power and domination.

When Sir Arthur Evans uncovered Knossos, he found to his surprise a kind of fairy palace, delicately ornamented, a storehouse of jewels and frescoes and painted reliefs. The arts of Knossos were rounded and complete. There was nothing hesitant. There was the sense of a people living in quiet enjoyment of life, loving the earth, enjoying bright colors and possessing exquisite taste, with an impressive serenity. There were no vast portraits of the gods; indeed, there were scarcely any gods, and the few that were discovered usually took the form of painted pottery figurines only a few inches high. The overwhelming impression produced by these discoveries was of a gay, sensual people innocent of any desire for war. The sea-raiders vanished; instead there were the young princes and princesses of the court nimbly leaping over the horns of bulls.

Thucydides tells how Minos sent his sons to rule over the Cyclades and put down piracy until he was the master of the seas, but he does not tell us how long the Minoan empire endured or how they maintained their power. Homer says there were a hundred cities in Crete, and many races lived in apparent harmony on the island at the time of the Trojan War. But of the religious beliefs of the people, and of their customs, neither Homer nor Thucydides tells us anything at all.

The archaeologists, confronted by the mystery, sometimes throw up their hands in despair. Dazzled by these people who left no decipherable writings except those brief lists of tribute scratched on clay which were deciphered by Michael Ventris, they tended to surrender to fantasy. Evans believed there was some mysterious connection between the rumblings of earthquakes and the bellowing of the sacred bulls. Pendlebury, who for years was Evans' assistant at Knossos, believed that Theseus succeeded in stealing the bull-mask from Minos before sacking the city and that they confronted one another in the throne room, the Greek conqueror disguised as a god and the only-too-human king. It is not strange that archaeologists in Crete should be continually devising fantasies. These fantasies seem to come out of the air unbidden, and as we traveled across Crete we found ourselves inventing them daily. Not far from Heracleion lies Mount Jouktas, carved like the sleeping face of a god. We seemed to see the sleeping and waking gods wherever we traveled.

Hagia Triada

On the south coast of Crete, looking toward Libya, there are the ruins of a small Minoan palace lying between the sea and snow-capped Mount Ida. No one knows the name of the site in Minoan times, and it is known today by the name of Hagia Triada, the Holy Trinity, from a Byzantine church which stands on the ridge overlooking the bay.

We drove across the island on one of those days when the sky is full of flickering blue flames and the earth basks quietly in the sun. There are stretches of the road as beautiful as the road from Rhodes to Lindos, the plains dappled with olive trees. A boy would ride past on a donkey, and suddenly the whole world would be revolving and dancing round the boy in intoxicated wonder; and so it was throughout the journey—the wonder and the dance. On a sunny day Crete is a country where simply to move along a road can be an intoxication.

Not far from the south coast lie the ruins of Gortyn, once a commercial capital with acres of marble temples, now a small village of perhaps twenty houses. Under the Romans it became the capital of Crete and of Cyrenaica, its governor ruling over all of North Africa between Egypt and Carthaginia. You wander over a field past a ruined Byzantine church to the remains of a small theater in a hollow, and there in a sheltered portico stands a wall inscribed with seventeen thousand Greek characters in "ox-turning" script. These are the laws of Gortyn, written about 500 B.C., deciding in vast detail questions of land and inheritance, murder, burglary, divorce, adultery, and a hundred other matters. The inscriptions run from left to right on the first line, then from right to left. Chickens peck at your feet. A small farm lies nearby, and the farmer's wife sees that the laws are regarded respectfully.

But there are more exciting things in Gortyn than the long wall engraved with laws. Across the fields on the other side of the road lie acres and acres of ruined walls, and the remains of long abandoned temples. Shrines and altars abound. Everything lies where it has fallen, as though a series of earthquakes had shaken buildings and columns down as easily as the wind shakes the leaves from a tree. In a sunken field in the shadow of olive trees there stands a headless goddess. She is Isis, the goddess of Egypt, a stranger to Greece.

The region of Hagia Triada is known as Paradise; it is well named. Suddenly everything is green, for the river Electra rushes wildly through a rich pastureland. Birds sing in the orchards, butterflies and dragonflies are everywhere, and the road to the Minoan palace is dark in the shade of fruit trees. Some boys came riding up on donkeys, offering to take us there, cavorting on a sandspit beside the river in their brilliant rags, and laughing when we explained we had already seen the palace and it was no more than four minutes' walk.

From Hagia Triada came many of the treasures in the museum at Heracleion: the painted sarcophagus of a young prince, the Harvester Vase, frescoes, jewels, and tablets inscribed in Linear A. It was a small palace, and may have been merely the seaside residence of the princes of Phaistos. The throne room faces the sea. There are courtyards, stairways, a theater, all in miniature. The palace lies on a ridge with a village below. A forest of pines, a white palace, the orchards and the sea. They had chosen well to live in Paradise.

Phaistos

From Hagia Triada it is only a short drive to Phaistos, the most impressive of all the Minoan palaces so far discovered. There may be other palaces hidden under crusts of earth, but it is unlikely that they will rival Phaistos for the perfect beauty of the site or for the sense of absolute power and domination which comes from those scarred and broken walls.

And yet, driving from Hagia Triada, there is nothing to prepare you for the spectacle of power, naked and brutal and yet somehow beautiful, which awaits you at Phaistos. The road winds along valleys under the soft southern sky, with silvery grey olive trees on either side, and there is a feeling of spaciousness such as you find nearly everywhere in Crete, though it is most noticeable near the southern coast. It is a land where nothing seems to be happening except the slow ripening of fruit trees. A few peasants work in the fields, the children riding on donkeyback are wild-eyed and rosy-cheeked, the villages are neat, and there are no factory chimneys. The earth cannot have changed very much in four thousand years. It is a quiet solemn landscape, very fertile, and there is nothing to suggest that these fields were battlegrounds. Some of the most terrible fighting during the Cretan uprisings against the Turks took place in these gently smiling fields.

Then, suddenly, up a stiff climb and around a bend, and you are in Phaistos, a city of giants.

Compared with Phaistos the royal villa at Hagia Triada is like a child's toy, and Gournia is a small pirate lair, and Knossos is a pleasant citadel. The palace looks down over the broad plain of Messara to the sea. Far away to the east like a puff of white smoke lies Dikte, to the north is Mount Ida with its telltale eye-patch of a cave, and to the south lie the Asterousia Mountains bordering the seacoast. Asterousia can only mean "starlit" or "starry," a pleasant name for a chain of sparkling mountains. There is a sense of breathtaking opulence in that view, with all the wealth of the world rolling at one's feet, though there is neither town nor village in sight.

Like a vast fortress-palace crowning the hill, Phaistos rides exuberantly over southern Crete. The ruins are bare and unornamented. There are no majestically carved Lion Gates, no fluted columns, no paintings of cupbearers and princes: only the unadorned shapes of palaces, courts, store rooms, dancing floors, places of sacrifice. One suspects that there was very little need of ornament at Phaistos. The great stairway, built of blocks up to nine feet long, is the purest monument. The sweep of it is insolent, contrived with deliberate grandeur. The masons knew exactly what they were doing and gave a camber to the stairway. The archaeologists will tell you that this is to permit rain-water to be channeled away, and the historians of Minoan culture will tell you that the prince of Phaistos walking in solemn procession down the stairway liked to appear taller than his retinue, but it is just as possible that the masons gave it a slight camber for the same reason that Doric columns are never straight, but have a slight swelling which conveys an impression of life and pleases the eye. The stairway was clearly intended to please.

Up this stairway came ambassadors to the court and the vassals of the prince of Phaistos bearing tribute offerings of immense jars of oil, wine and grain, later to be stored in the palace strong rooms. The jars remain, some of them so tall that it is impossible to peer into them without the use of the terracotta stools which have been found nearby. The stairs are shallow, only about two inches high, and the tribute-bearers, a dozen to a jar, would have little difficulty in carrying up their offerings. The jars have the familiar rope pattern cut into them. It must be the oldest surviving pattern, for fishermen in Crete still use jars carved with the same pattern.

Beyond the stairway lie the ruined walls, an immense complex of rooms, some of them nearly as small as the rooms in Gournia which would be crowded if more than two people sat in them. The doorways are narrow slits. The roofs have gone, but the rooms are uncomfortably airless even without roofs, and must have been stifling in the heat of summer. It is a reasonable assumption that the Minoans spent most of their lives in the open air.

In Phaistos there are none of the extraneous decorations to be found at Knossos: no scarlet concrete pillars hold up the roofs, no frescoes adorn the walls, no horns of consecration and patterned shields and double axes are to be seen. Phaistos is naked power in all its majesty.

The Birth of Zeus

Hesiod in the *Theogony* tells how Zeus at his birth was in danger of being swallowed by his father Cronus, and was therefore spirited away at night to a remote cave in Crete under thickly wooded

Mount Aigaios. He grew up under the care of the nymph Amalthea and the Curetes, warrior gods who sang songs in his honor accompanied by a wild stamping of feet. Amalthea, who seems to have been a goat-goddess, suckled him with goat's milk, while the Curetes saw that he grew up into a sturdy youth. For the Cretans Zeus was always youthful; the Greeks saw him as eternally wise and old.

All over Crete there are caves, and not all authorities are agreed that the cave of Dikte is the authentic birthplace. Yet since Roman times there has been a fair agreement that Zeus was born there. What is certain is that if a great and powerful god must be born in a cave, he would choose well to be born in Dikte.

It is a long and roundabout journey over bad roads to the village of Psychro, which clings to a shoulder of the mountain high above the plain of Lasithi festooned with windmills. Psychro is a typical mountain village consisting of two streets, and the cave is a hard twenty minutes' walk up the mountain. The air is pure. Thick gorse covers the mountainside, and as you follow the winding path, watching the mountain ahead for every glimpse of a fissure, of some magic opening into a mysterious cavern, you see nothing to suggest that it is anything but a very ordinary mountain. For some reason I thought the cave would be quite small, perhaps the size of a three-story house. The guide, who carried candles, said it would take four or five hours to see all the chambers in the cave, and I began to revise my opinions about its size. Suddenly we came to a small opening about four feet wide. "Here is the cave," the guide said, and we looked at him in disbelief.

When we had slithered down ten feet of mud and rubble, and he had lit the candles, we saw we were in a cave about the size of a cathedral. Vast shadows loomed. There was no pathway. It was icy cold, and very damp. We jumped from rock to rock, making our way down a steep and sometimes precipitous slope, and all the time it grew colder. The faint candlelight flickered on the vast overarching roof of the cave. Down below there were lakes, huge stalagmites like the gnarled tree trunks of a forest entirely made of ice, and little grottoes formed of ice. One of the stalagmites was broken. "A German soldier came here during the war and threw a hand grenade at it," the guide said, and went on to curse all Germans. Here and there were curious shelves like altars. It was on these shelves that offerings were laid in ancient times, to be found by Evans and Halbsherr at the beginning of this century. And strangely there was no sense of being in a cave; instead, there was the sense of being in some vast building constructed out of rock and ice, and deliberately designed.

Archaeologists in Crete are continually devising fantasies. On the way out of the cave, lurching zigzag among the frozen rocks, I devised one more fantasy. It seemed to me that the labyrinth, which appears on Cretan coins and in so many legends, was simply the portrait of the labyrinthine cave of Zeus.

The Cave of Eileithyia

There was a time when from all over the Greek world women came to bring offerings to the cave of Eileithyia. This goddess with the name like rippling water may have been the most ancient of the goddesses, having come to birth long before Zeus and Hera ruled over Olympus. Hesiod says she was the daughter of Zeus by Hera, and Ares the war god was her brother, but everything we know about her suggests a more ancient ancestry. Her home was a small cave on a hillside overlooking the sea. From that dark cave among the stalagmites she gave comfort to women in childbirth.

There are caves all over Crete, but there was no other so beloved by women. How famous it was we know from the lips of Odysseus who, returning to Ithaca in disguise, amused himself by telling Penelope he was a Cretan who had encountered Odysseus long ago "at Amnisos where the cave of Eileithyia is." She was a goddess before Apollo was born, for she was summoned to attend his birth, and we learn that Leto "threw her arms round a palm tree and braced her knees against the soft grass while the earth cried for joy beneath her." It was due to Eileithyia that the birth was so easy.

So they represented her as a young woman naked and kneeling, for Greek women customarily gave birth on their knees, and they placed a dove in one of her hands and a torch in the other to signify that she brought children into the light of day. They told few legends about her, perhaps because she had no need of legends. It was enough that she was always there, giving women the comfort they desired.

Today only a few countrywomen go to that cave, remembering the goddess who reigned there long before King Minos and the Trojan wars. There are no shrines or altars to the goddess; there is only the darkness of the small cave sloping into the underbelly of the earth and the sudden gleam of stalagmites in torchlight. Outside the cave mouth a stunted fig tree, the symbol of love and fertility, leans against the wind. Amnisos has vanished. Odysseus called it "a difficult harbor," but it is difficult no longer, and no longer a harbor. All that remains of Amnisos is a great terraced mound jutting out to sea, and the stairway leading up the hillside to the cave has long since vanished. From Amnisos Idomeneus, Prince of Crete, grandson of King Minos and Queen Pasiphaë, set sail for Troy.

Along a winding road three miles east of the municipal airport there is a small wooden marker pointing in the direction of the cave. You could easily overlook the marker, and having found it and clambered down the hillside you could easily overlook the cave hidden by its guardian fig tree. You slither down a short slope, make your way through an opening scarcely wide enough for two people to walk abreast, and at once you are in a vast echoing cavern of slippery rock. That is what it seems to be. In fact, it is a very ordinary cave, and what appears at first to be a vast chamber becomes no more than a broad gallery with a bellying roof, and there is a kind of altar, and a broken stalagmite which authorities on ancient Cretan customs are disposed to regard as a holy lingam; but I fail to see how a lingam can help a woman in childbirth. There are more stalagmites as you penetrate deeper into the cave; they crowd together and barely permit the passage of an intruder. Fifty feet from the mouth the cave with its monstrous shadows comes abruptly to an end.

It is a damp and depressing place, and by no stretch of the imagination is it possible to believe that any charismatic quality still lingers in it. Once there was an officiating priestess, candles glowed, incantations were chanted, and perhaps lambs were slaughtered, and the women prayed for easy births and their prayers were granted. Eileithyia was a kindly goddess, and she had no need for a vast palace. The cave of Dikte, where Zeus was born, towers to the height of a cathedral; Eileithyia lives in her small house, dispensing kindness rather than mercy as she brings children into the light. She could be reached by a steep but not very long walk from Amnisos, and the walk itself, undertaken slowly, perhaps helped to bring about the easy birth for which the women prayed. The very ordinariness of the cave may have been comforting.

The rock was slippery, for there were lakes of mud formed by centuries of spring rains. The shelving roof and bulging walls were shapeless and comfortless in the light of the flaming rolled-up newspapers we were using to explore the cave, but soon it became evident that there was nothing to explore. Deep inside the cave we found a few pieces of ancient pottery, perhaps the remnants of votive offerings, but there were no designs on the pottery, nothing to show its age.

So the cave was disappointing, and at the same time oddly pleasing for the very reason that it was disappointing. Of all the shrines in the world this cave has the longest continuous history, for women still go there as they have been going since neolithic times, and it is wholly without decoration, empty. Perhaps it was always empty, perhaps emptiness was what the women desired; and just as at Eleusis the mystery of life was shown in an ear of wheat, so at the cave of Eileithyia the mystery of birth was shown in an empty cave by the seashore.

The rolled-up newspapers had burned away, as we made our way toward the dim bluish light of the narrow opening. Suddenly we heard a strange sound like distant hoofbeats. There had been a gust of wind, and a few ripe figs were falling into the echoing cave.

The Silver Coin

By day we would find ourselves traveling across Crete, to Phaistos and Dikte and beyond, but always in the evenings we found
ourselves in Heracleion. It is not a town of any great beauty, and
once you have seen the archaeological museum and the old Venetian fort reached by a long jetty, there is little left to see. The shops
are tawdry, most of the hotels look as though they were put up
yesterday and will fall tomorrow, and the government buildings
look like slabs of concrete. Decidedly Heracleion is not a town
which invites a long stay.

Here and there, especially in the evening, there are glimpses of a
vanished beauty. The old Venetian fort with the lion of St. Mark
riding proudly over its gates lives on in mournful quietness, serving
no purpose now that the last cannon have been taken down. The
Germans mounted machine guns on these turret walls during the
last war, and any caïque which sailed into the harbor would have to
declare itself or be riddled with bullets. Now the fort is abandoned,
and only the lovers come to the jetty in the evening, while the
seagulls cry mournfully.

Mournful is the word for Heracleion, mournful the streets,
mournful the great Venetian walls which enclose the town as a
perpetual reminder of a former glory, mournful the narrow winding
alleyway, mournful the shops and the cinemas playing twenty-year-
old films, mournful the food, and most mournful of all the wine. So
mournful a place that it was always a delight to hurry away early in
the morning to the freshness of the great plains and the blue moun-

tains and the villages where the men were apple-cheeked and still wore the ancient Cretan costume.

Sometimes in the evening, oppressed by a sense of fury, we would find ourselves stalking up King Constantine Street to examine once more the fly-blown cinema posters of an earlier age or the shop windows filled with gimcrack snake goddesses, minotaurs and princes of Knossos, all made in Germany or Japan, and all made badly, so that they had only a distant resemblance to the clearcut originals in the archaeological museum. There were models of the Parthenon, heads of Nefertiti, more double axes than we could count. One would have thought there would be no great difficulty in making a reasonable facsimile of a double ax, but the double axes all looked wrong, and so did the heads of Nefertiti, and so did the Parthenon. The windows were crammed with imitations of ancient art, and they proved only that ancient art was inimitable.

If the shop windows were horrors, there were greater horrors within. At the rear of the shops there was always a rickety wooden ladder leading to a kind of loft where the most secret treasures were kept. Here, at a price, you are offered the authentic jewels found by private archaeological expeditions. Jewels worn in the Minoan court, delicate butterflies pricked out in gold filigree, medallions engraved with leaping bulls, double axes hammered out in thin gold, together with the figurines which adorned their altars, are sold over the counter. They are wrapped in tissue and cotton. The shopkeeper's hand trembles as he displays them, and his voice drops to a whisper as he explains that this is all contraband, brought secretly to Heracleion by the private archaeologists who prefer that these treasures belong to the world rather than to the crowded museums. The Greek government does not know, will never know. The shopkeeper offers you tea and asks whether you are interested in icons painted by Damaskinos and El Greco, and finally with vast ceremony and infinite caution the ancient icons are unwrapped and laid reverently on the table. They are very faded, but the signatures are clear and freshly painted. If the icons do not please you, there remains a collection of ancient bronze figures adorned with serpentine phalluses, and as he unwraps them, he nudges your arm and invites you to partake at a distance of three thousand years in an ancient fertility rite. If neither Minoan bulls nor snake goddesses nor icons nor bronze figurines please you, he will display a forest of matchboxes each containing a rare and otherwise unprocurable Cretan coin.

Sometimes no doubt someone falls for the bait, for the atmosphere is properly conspiratorial. How pleasant to buy an authentic El Greco! How delightful to possess a necklace once worn by a Minoan princess! How charming to outwit the police! But unfortunately not one of the objects lying in their cocoons of cotton was more than a few years old. The El Grecos, the gold butterflies, the double axes, the bulls, the necklaces and even the coins were clumsy fakes, and all seemed to come from the same factory. The coins were lumpish, the bronze boys with the serpentine phalluses looked oddly like storm troopers, and the artist who modeled the gilded butterfly had originally set out to portray an elephant and changed his mind at the last moment. We yearned for a passable fake. If only there had been a single Cretan coin which did not look obviously wrong! Surely it was possible to find an authentic piece somewhere in that triumphal procession of fakes! But there were none.

We pretended to show interest in some of the pieces and were suitably rewarded. The El Greco with the paint still wet on the signature was two thousand dollars. For five hundred dollars we could buy an ithyphallic storm trooper guaranteed to have been dug up at Knossos. The golden butterfly was cheaper. He seemed to have little confidence in the coins and was prepared to sacrifice them for about fifty dollars each. We were told that few people were interested in coins and they did not sell as well as the storm troopers.

The long interview over, we would descend the creaking staircase, voicing our infinite regrets. A new sewer was being laid in King Constantine Street, and in the darkness we would make our way dangerously to the sea-front or to the winding roads beneath the Venetian wall where sometimes a street lamp glimmering on an old house or a heraldic emblem carved over a doorway would hint at a time when Venetian grandees ruled and never guessed that a greater empire than theirs had ruled over the eastern Mediterranean from a city only a few miles away.

One evening, when we were wandering disconsolately round the Morosini fountain, going slowly mad with the boredom of our evenings which had come to resemble dull hammerblows, I said something about the pure pleasure of coming upon a relic of ancient Greece, a small statue, a lamp, a coin, anything at all. Alexander hinted darkly that anything we came upon would be a fake, even if we dug for it ourselves and pulled it out of the ground. Fakes were everywhere. Probably half the objects in the museums were fakes. Knossos itself was a fake invented by Sir Arthur Evans. The red jars of Mallia were *not* fakes, and we allowed that *La Parisienne* was an authentic painting from an authentic palace in Knossos, but we had become connoisseurs of fakery, our eagle eyes sharpened by

too long an acquaintance with King Constantine Street. So we de-
bated frivolously, walking giddily round the fountain. The shops
were closing. It was growing late. There was a small shop selling
antiques across the road—it was one of the few we had not visited
—and we decided to look at some more fakes, to listen with an air
of enchantment to the spiel of the shopkeeper and to watch with
bated breath while he unwrapped his treasures. We were masochists
in search of punishment: it was the price we paid for our con-
noisseurship.

The shopkeeper was a man of about thirty, who resembled a
gently humorous young professor. He was dressed in somber black,
and his long lean face would sometimes settle into an expression of
mourning, but there were puckers of amusement around his eyes.
He unwrapped his treasures. They were the usual fakes. We rejoiced exceedingly as he lifted them out of their cocoons and held
them with exactly the proper reverence suitable for ancient things.
He showed us his collection of coins. It was a terrible collection,
though rather more impressive than the lumps in King Constantine
Street because they were all electrotypes and therefore accurate
copies of the originals. There was not a single authentic coin in the
collection.

He shrugged his shoulders.

"I know they are electrotypes," he said. "They are not worth
anything."

This startled us. For the first time we met a shopkeeper in
Heracleion who did not attach a preposterous value to fakes.

Then he said: "A peasant brought in a coin last week. He said he
dug it up in his field, but that's what they always say. Would you
like to see it?"

The coin was in a little tin box among nails, thumb tacks and paper clips, where it had been lying ever since the peasant came in with it.

"You can't trust the peasants," the shopkeeper went on. "They come every day. They bring fakes all the time, and we have to send them away. God knows where they get them from!"

Angelic shopkeeper, so accustomed to fakes that he could not recognize an authentic work of art! The coin was not a fake. It was not an electrotype. It was not hammered into shape by someone in a backstreet in Heracleion. Like *La Parisienne* it spoke with absolute authority of a great age in art, now vanished, never to be imitated. A goddess lay among the thumb tacks, her brooding, gentle face no more than an inch high. Nevertheless she filled the whole room with her divine presence.

On one side of the didrachm was Demeter, veiled and wreathed with corn, grave and austere, with features of classic beauty. On the reverse there appeared to be a sailor steering his ship and the letters KTIO. Time had rubbed the sailor smooth, but the goddess was brilliantly preserved, her thick curls sharply etched, with delicate wisps of hair about the ears. She was all grace and dignity, while lost in thought, her troubled gaze settled upon the day when her daughter Persephone would be returned to her. She was the oldest of the living goddesses, mother of the earth and all its fruits, and therefore all the more precious.

We carried Demeter with us during our travels, and sometimes we would find ourselves wondering about the sailor from the mysterious land of Ktio, which does not appear on maps of Greece or the islands. We came to the conclusion that it was one of those islands which had been submerged by volcanic eruption like San-

torin, and where once there were lemon groves and marble altars
sacred to Demeter, there were only seagulls. In its brief life Ktio
had been famous for its sheltered ports and the magnificent daring
of its sailors. On this island there was no death, and Persephone
never vanished from the sight of her mother.

Alas for Ktio! The enchanted island lived in our imaginations for
the space of a week. Returning to Athens, we discovered that the
sailor, who seemed to be leaning on the prow of a ship, was really
Apollo leaning on his lyre. The coin had been struck by order of
King Philip of Macedon in 346 B.C. to celebrate his tyranny over
Greece as leader of the Amphiktionic League. Ktio was not an
island; it was merely a part of the word Amphiktion engraved in
three places around the coin. A careless die-stamper had cut off
half the word.

We had lost an island, but we gained Apollo. The artist had
shown him in a moment of profound meditation, one hand lifted to
his face, the other grasping a laurel bough. He sits on his royal
throne at Delphi, the omphalos which marks the center of the
world, a strange egg-shaped throne decorated with a net of woolen
fillets, and because the laurel bough signifies purification, he is
present as the god of purity, and because he rests his elbow on his
lyre and wears the long white citharoedic robe, he is also present as
the god of music. So he dreams and meditates, pondering the birth
of sunlit worlds and all the works of the imagination, the sweetest
and purest of the gods. It was strange to find him with Demeter
among the thumb tacks.

The Grave of Nikos Kazantzakis

The Greek imagination is still haunted by ancient tragedies. Most of the novelists and poets of modern Greece seem to be fleeing from the avenging furies of the past. They cannot escape from Homer, the great tragedians, or Pindar. They are in the unenviable position of knowing that whatever they say has already been said before. The past weighs heavily on them and crushes them.

Not even Nikos Kazantzakis, one of the few authentic geniuses produced by modern Greece, was able to avoid the tyranny of the past. He wrote three masterpieces: *Zorba the Greek, Freedom or Death,* and *The Greek Passion,* and a vast amount of erratic journalism. He wandered over most of the world, a small, precise, tortured and kindly man consumed with an abiding love of humanity and intolerant of most of the people he met in his travels. He adored swashbucklers, but was happiest in his library; and loved children, and died childless after two marriages. He was Don Odysseus, always tilting at windmills and setting off for an unattainable Ithaca. He studied philosophy under Bergson in Paris, and went on to study most of the arts known to the world, but the ancient Greek past held him by the throat and all his writings are saturated with the thoughts of men living nearly twenty-five centuries ago. His tragedies are ancient Greek tragedies, and his monumental poem called *The Odyssey, A Modern Sequel,* which runs to thirty-five thousand lines, could have been written by an Alexandrian poet living in the age of the Ptolemies. He tried to break out of the iron chain by brute force, but never succeeded. He was an ancient Greek living in our own age.

Kazantzakis was born in Heracleion, but though he loved the city he spent very little time there. The house where he is supposed to have been born is still standing, but there is some doubt whether it is in fact his birthplace. In the grubby historical museum, dark with nineteenth-century paintings and bright with the curved swords used by the Greeks during their war of independence, a special room has been set aside for his books and manuscripts. You can see the simple black-painted table where he worked, his spittoon, his walking sticks, his umbrella, his pen and inkwell, and all those other memorabilia which a pious posterity preserves. The room is supposed to be an exact reproduction of his study; one hopes it is nothing of the kind, for it is dismally barren and the only color comes from a shelf of yellow French paperbacks tattered with age. It is almost a relief to return to the fly-specked paintings and the endless sword-blades. Schoolchildren patter dutifully along the corridors of the museum, their voices echoing in an empty house. They are ushered into the room where the works of Kazantzakis are preserved under glass and listen attentively to the lecturer who explains that it was on that table in that room, or in a very similar room, that the masterpieces were written; and the children look blank, for the man is no longer there and his ghost has fled.

The tables of writers make good firewood. I suspect that Kazantzakis would have hated that room, so bleak and uninviting. He cared very little for the physical things of life, and cared least of all for houses. He belonged to the open air.

When he died in 1957, a few months before his seventy-fifth birthday, from a deadly infection brought about by a clumsy doctor in Peking who gave him a smallpox inoculation with an unsterilized syringe, Heracleion claimed him. He had hoped to be buried

quietly; instead he was buried with fanfare on the great Fortinengo
bastion of the old Venetian wall. It is a wonderful place, high up
above the city, the air sweet and pure with the fragrance of the
plains. The top of the bastion is as large as a small park, and in the
middle lies the grave of rough-hewn local stone. A wooden Cross
stands before it, suggesting that he was a man of grave orthodoxy.
In fact he was a pagan to the end, and the inscription he ordered to
be carved on his tombstone reads:

> *I hope for nothing.*
> *I fear nothing.*
> *I am free.*

It is strange to come there, in that quietness, and to see a war
going on. In June 1963, six years after his death, the grave was
dynamited and the inscription destroyed. A new inscription was
engraved in bronze, and the Greek Orthodox Church, which had
refused to bury him with full rites, replied by erecting the Cross
within a few inches of his proud claim. There was to be no peace
for Kazantzakis dead or alive.

So the war goes on: the pagan defiantly shouting from the graves
that he hopes for nothing, and the Church protesting silently that
all men need the promise of the Cross. The Church in Greece is
weary of paganism. The words of Kazantzakis are clichés. "I was
not; I came to be; I am not; I care not"—these words appear on a
thousand ancient Greek tombs. Kazantzakis was merely exercising
his right to die like an ancient Greek.

They buried him like a pagan king on the heights overlooking the
city. Mount Jouktas, sharp-edged against the heavens, shaped like

the face of sleeping Zeus, looks down on him, the sea lies below. There is grandeur in that lonely burial place. Alive, he was a thorn in the flesh of the Greeks. Dead, he became part of the protecting wall of the town he loved best.

It is good to stand there and to see the red roofs spread out before you, and to taste the clean winds and to enjoy the silence. The lizards sun themselves on the tomb, and the Cross like a sundial throws its long shadow over the rough stone and the letters of bronze. Meanwhile the war goes on. Sooner or later someone will come with another stick of dynamite.

Santorin

NOT AGAIN in this life do I expect to see an island so ghostly as Santorin—so ghostly and so hauntingly beautiful. I remember that during the afternoon the air gave an impression of mistiness: not that there was any visible mist, but the air had thickened and was dyed a deeper blue than the air over Heracleion, which we had left the previous evening. It rarely takes an effort to look at Greece; now there was a sense of effort as the eye had to strike deeper through the weight of air to see the island in the distance, blue turrets low down on the horizon, veiled in a kind of mist, and strangely exciting. Perhaps it was simply the name of the island which lent excitement to those small blue turrets, or their ancient legends. Otherwise it was difficult to understand why the whole forward part of the ship was crowded with passengers who watched in silence, as though under a spell.

They had not crowded the deck when we sailed into Heracleion, although they were tourists and might be expected to look at Crete with a sense of wonder and expectation. They would have their one day in Crete and most of it would be spent at Knossos and in the curio shops on King Constantine Street; Crete was something they knew about. Santorin was something else altogether, with no great island history, and there were no curio shops. Its history was to be measured by volcanic explosions and in periodic flames which leaped from the bottom of the ocean. Everyone knew it was a strange island, which did not obey any of the laws generally assumed to apply to the islands. So they leaned against the rails and peered through the thickening air at the gay little turrets low on the horizon, which were not in themselves remarkable and seemed designed to mislead the traveler into thinking that after all Santorin might be like all the other islands.

At this distance, with Santorin still five or six miles away, we began to wonder whether we might not be sailing toward some other island altogether. The turrets became two blue hills, not notably volcanic. We had expected outlying islands, white churches on the summits, cliffs the color of flame. A friend who was born in Santorin had said in Athens: "Wait till you see Santorin. Do you know what the ancient Greeks called it? *Kallisté*—the most beautiful." He went on to say that it was twenty years since he had been on the island, but he remembered it every night in his dreams. "Is it so very beautiful?" we asked, turning over the pages of a travel folder with a picture of a white church, which seemed to be the same white church we had seen on many other travel folders. "Wait till you see it," he said, and went on to talk about the new exhibition of Byzantine art then being shown in Athens.

Wait till you see it! But we were still waiting, while the island drew closer, always misty blue, and looking like any other island seen at random. This was certainly not *kallisté,* and we went on to discuss the ideal island, which would have an acropolis perched on a cliff like Lindos, and a ruined agora with the columns still standing like Thasos, and somewhere there would be a stairway like the great stairway at Phaistos. There would be flowers in abundance, and a vast number of statues still standing where they had been erected. Alexander had a passion for photographing fishing boats, especially red ones, and so we inserted a yellow beach and a small fishing harbor. Later we made various emendations and corrections to the ideal island, finally giving it the wonderful Apollonian gateway which stands on Naxos. On the island of Syra there are two peaks overlooking the harbor with the Orthodox Church sitting on one peak and the Roman Catholic Church on the other; we found such symmetry commendable, and henceforward the ideal island possessed twin peaks. Meanwhile Santorin was coming closer, still blue, still misty, still shapeless. The passengers were still bending over the rails and peering wordlessly into the distance. Binoculars were being exchanged. The excitement was mounting.

Now one by one the blue humps and turrets began to disintegrate and change color. There was Great Burnt Island and Little Burnt Island, and these were brown and low on the water; Therasia was blue, and this island together with one of the arms of Santorin had formed the blue turrets we had seen in the distance. It is only when you have entered the fantastic bay, rounding the headlands, that Santorin appears for the first time in its fiery beauty. For there, rising sheer from the sea, was the scarlet cliff layered here and there with jeweled strands of emerald and ruby, with the white city basking on its summit.

The gate of the temple of Apollo at Naxos.

Poppies and olive trees at Lesbos.

The Straits of Samos, with Cape Mycale in the distance.

Naxos from the sea.

Santorin from the sea.

The heights of Santorin.

A church on the waterfront at Paros.

Looking out from the temple of Athena Lindia at Lindos.

It was so strange a cliff, so vividly colored, that at first you can scarcely bring yourself to believe in its existence. It is like a backdrop painted by an artist who has gone completely out of his wits. This beetling cliff seems to hang suspended in space; a single puff might blow it over. Then gradually as you grow accustomed to that savage mountain, you realize that you are a thousand feet deep within the crater of a volcano which has exploded many times and will no doubt explode many more times. Vesuvius has come to the Aegean Sea.

In historical times there have been about twenty volcanic eruptions at Santorin. Strabo records an eruption which took place in 196 B.C., when "flames and smoke rose from the seabed for four days and nights, causing the whole of it to boil and be on fire." In 726 A.D. another island appeared in the bay. Little Burnt Island emerged in 1570. Great Burnt Island appeared in 1707. As late as 1956 there was a series of earthquakes which reduced the town of Pyrgos to rubble. But it is not for these minor eruptions and disturbances that Santorin is remembered by historians. What chiefly interests the historians is the great eruption which took place about 1520 B.C., causing a tidal wave which swept across Crete sixty miles to the south and extinguished the powerful Minoan empire. Only once in historical times has there been an eruption of such intensity and destructive power. This took place on the island of Krakatoa in the East Indies in 1887, and produced tidal waves fifty feet high, destroying towns hundreds of miles away.

Santorin, then, is the cup which held the deadly poison, the destroyer of an entire civilization. Even now it has the appearance of being red-hot, glowing with volcanic flame.

From the tourist ship anchored in the bay a quarter of a mile offshore, you can make out the white mule track climbing the nearly vertical cliff in fierce zigzags; it looks absurdly uninviting until, reaching the shore by caïque, you see the crowd of small mules preparing to make the ascent. The mules are unblinkered; they have high wooden saddles securely strapped, and look peaceful and gentle enough. It is only later as you begin to climb the endless road that you begin to realize that the people of Santorin are not joking when they say the mules are inhabited by the souls of the damned. They are weary of carrying people up that terrible cliff and would like to throw off their burdens once and for all. They have long practiced their nefarious trade and they can gauge to a hairbreadth the weaknesses of their riders. They know how to lurch, to sprint, to gallop, to leap frenziedly against the sea-wall in the hope that the rider will come unstuck from the saddle and hurtle over the scarlet cliff, to be dashed to pieces on the rock below. They know how to inspire fear and they accomplish their purpose with quiet deliberation.

I rode up the cliff on the most beautiful mule I have ever seen. It was a pale misty white, and resembled the mules which appear in Italian paintings of the visit of the Three Magi to Bethlehem. The head was wonderfully sculptured; it moved with delicacy and precision. Nevertheless it twice galloped against the cliff wall in a determined effort to brush me off its back, and three times it lunged against the low wall built to protect the unwary traveler from plunging over the side. At such moments I found myself hanging in space with a prodigious view of vertiginous cliffs and the distant sea, which looked altogether too impassive and calm. The white cruise ship was merely a dot on the wrinkled sea.

I cursed the mule and all its works, cursed Santorin, and went on to curse myself for my folly in entrusting my life to a mule so beautiful that I should have known it was damned. I had no interest in Santorin when we reached the top of the cliff. For all I cared, it could erupt again and throw up another tidal wave, and take me with it. The muleteer was giving some hay to the mule, which was munching contentedly.

But on those heights, on firm ground, reason gradually asserts itself and curses die away in the thin air. The town, which looked like a dazzling snowfall from the sea, was still dazzling. Two streets ran along the bony spine, and the white houses vied with one another as to which could reach out further over the cliffs. The lanes were narrow, silent, muffled, so that the sound of one's own footsteps resembled the tramp of armies. A square opens out, then closes again, and there is only the narrow ridge along the edge of the cliff. Out of this white silence a boy emerged with a piece of bright pink pumice which he held up as though it was some strange jewel, for it glinted unbearably in the brilliant light. I offered to pay for it, but he merely smiled and thrust it in my hands, and vanished down a white lane.

The Catholics have been a powerful force in Santorin ever since the islands fell to the Crusaders in 1204. The Catholic cathedral stands with its white towers for all the world as though it had been set down in some plain in Italy, though it is perched on the edge of the cliffs. Inside, candles were burning before the altar and the air was thick with incense. Coming out of the cathedral into the thin washed air of Santorin was to leap from the Christian West into the white and silent world of the East. One could imagine hooded Moroccans walking through those muffled streets more easily than those deep-chested handsome peasant boys on donkeys.

Santorin has an excellent small museum which consists of two rooms, one of them being a basement where the treasures are kept in storage. The most valuable treasures are the geometric vases four and five feet high, but there are also a number of archaic kouroi discovered by Baron Hiller von Gaertringen who excavated the site of Thera, the ancient capital of the island, at his own expense.

Hiller was enchanted by ancient Thera chiefly because it was known that the youths who took part in the festivals of Apollo had inscribed on the walls of the sanctuary of the god their love messages to one another. "Ariston is beautiful." "Eumelos is the finest dancer." These venerable graffiti dated from the eighth century before Christ, and were unknown elsewhere, although there are indications that a similar custom was practiced in Athens. The inscriptions bearing the names of handsome boys are recorded at vast length in four massive volumes which Hiller published at the turn of the century. Unfortunately they tell us little more than the inscriptions discovered in the Minoan palaces in Crete: they amount only to a catalogue of boys.

Out of ancient Thera sailed the expeditions which settled Cyrene on the African coast. Herodotus tells the story of how Grinos, king of Thera, consulted the Delphic oracle and was ordered to found a colony in Libya; and not knowing where Libya was, and not caring to venture abroad, he disobeyed the oracle. For seven years no rain fell on the island, and the trees died. At last, fearing the wrath of the god, he set off for Libya in two fifty-oared galleys with his chosen companions, but when he reached the coast of Africa he felt sure the oracle had made a mistake and set sail for Thera again, abandoning the enterprise. The islanders refused to let him land. Once more he set out for Libya, and on a small island off the coast he founded a colony which did not prosper. Two years passed. The settlers suffered from hunger and loneliness. They abandoned the island and made their way to Delphi, to ask the god once more what he intended of them, and received the stern reply that they had been disobedient and would be punished unless they obeyed the law of Apollo, who commanded them to settle in Africa, not to take possession of a small island off the coast of Africa. So for the third time they set sail, and at last founded the colony of Cyrene, naming it after a girl who in Apollo's presence fought singlehandedly against a lion. Cyrene, founded in 631 B.C., grew to become an empire. "You are a king over great cities, and this great privilege is a shining heritage of your house," wrote Pindar in an ode addressed to King Arcesilaus of Cyrene in 462 B.C. In time Cyrene mounted an army and threatened Egypt, and its fame was so great that the kingdom was mentioned in a monument set up by King Asoka in India. The small volcanic island had given birth to a string of cities on the north coast of Africa; the daughter was greater than the mother.

Today there is no vestige of imperial grandeur on Santorin. There is the grandeur of the sheer cliffs, the white city, the pure and naked air on the towering heights. Here you have the feeling that you are living in the skies, remote from the earth and from the preoccupations of men. It is a strange and enchanted world, and perhaps dangerous:

> *A savage place! As holy and enchanted*
> *As e'er beneath a waning moon was haunted . . .*

Delos

WHEN DELOS SWIMS into the early morning light, grey and misty and damp with the night dews, you would think you are coming to a small abandoned quarry, an island of broken stones; and even when the sun rises, it is so barren an island, and so shapeless, with no mountains and valleys to give it form, that you would think it was a desert set in the middle of the Aegean. At high noon Delos comes into its own. Then the stones glitter and pour out a white radiance which meets the reflected radiance from the marble islands around. The sky becomes a triumphal archway of light, and then at last you come to realize why this small, low-lying island, the birthplace of Apollo, was so sacred to the Greeks.

Delos, then, is this strange shining high up in the air, the flashing of pure light, the beating of mysterious wings. This light is never still, but quivers and pulsates, flashing off sea and rock and marble with furious intensity. The island lies at the center of the Cyclades, with the other islands circling around it, but it is only on Delos that there is this pure concentration of light. Because the light was so beautiful, it became the birthplace of the god of light.

At first the island hesitated before accepting a god who was so arrogant and powerful that he threatened to unseat the gods of Olympus. The *Homeric Hymn to Delian Apollo* tells of the island's complaint against the coming of the god:

> *How shall I receive the god, the proud one,*
> *The arrogant one who stands in the highest place*
> *Above all the gods and people of the teeming earth?*
> *My heart is fearful at the thought of his coming,*
> *But when he sees me at the first leap of the sunrise*
> *Surely he will despise me, a heap of barren stones!*
> *He will press his foot on me, he will thrust me*
> *Into the waves of the sea, and the waves will wash over me,*
> *And then he will turn away into another place*
> *And build his temples in a land of fruitful trees,*
> *And I shall be lost in the dark sea. Only the black seals*
> *And the octopuses shall live on me . . .*

The island relented or grew less fearful, and when Apollo was born, she welcomed him with open arms. She had little to give him—marshes, crags, reefs, a small hill. In time the Greeks built more palaces, temples, porticoes and colonnades on this island than anywhere else except for the vast complex of shrines and sanctuaries at Delphi, which was also sacred to Apollo. The barren island, three miles long, a mile wide, became his perpetual shrine, and from all over Greece pilgrims came with offerings. Like Asclepius,

who was his son, he was a god of the healing arts, and therefore
they came with their prayers, begging to be cured, but his empire
extended far beyond the healing arts. He was the god of the sun, of
song and music, of prophecy, of the foundation of cities, and he
was the protector of flocks. The bright radiance of the Greek mind
was a reflection of his beauty. He was the light which quickens the
spirit.

Now there are only the shattered ruins—the ruins which belong
properly to Apollo, and the others which belong to the gods he
shielded and permitted to dwell with him: Isis, Hadad, Atargatis,
and even more mysterious gods from Syria. Apollo was so tolerant,
his power so immense that he could afford the luxury of strangers.
No one was left in any doubt that the island belonged to him. On
the sacred lake the swans of Apollo steeped their heads in the holy
water beneath a row of lionesses carved from Naxian marble; and
as the swans were sacred to Apollo, the lionesses were sacred to his
sister Artemis. Originally there were fourteen; now only five remain, and there is a sixth guarding the arsenal at Venice, having
been removed at the end of the seventeenth century.

These lionesses are very young, crouched on their haunches,
waiting to spring. The long, lean flanks taper like bullets, and they
have even in their archaic stillness a murderous look about them.
They would tear to pieces anyone who offended the goddess. The
peaceful swans circled the lake, and the lionesses kept watch.

The Sanctuary of Apollo

The sun came hot over the island, burning into the rock until in the midsummer stillness you could hear the rock-face creaking in the heat, the pale grey flakes of silvery mica cracking and falling away, blowing off like thistledown, as they have done each summer day over the centuries. The heat on Delos is a thing to strike terror in the heart. It comes in pulsating waves, and as noon approaches each wave seems brighter and fiercer than the last, burning deeper into the rock, the flesh, the soil. At noon poor naked Delos is the ravished bride of the sun.

In that heat one walks slowly, taking what little shelter there is along the pathways between the ruins, where only the brown and black lizards dart. They are the ugliest lizards I have ever seen, shapeless and mottled, with no grace in them; perched on the ancient marble columns, they watch menacingly. They are heavier and squatter than the lizards on the other islands, and belong, it would seem, to a species prevalent only on Delos and some regions of North Africa. Among the titles of Apollo was that of "Lizard-slayer." Evidently he did not kill enough of them. They own the island, and the rest of us are only interlopers.

Soon enough from the shore you come to the sanctuary of Apollo, a great square of littered ruins set among wild thistles and barley grass with scarcely anything standing above waist height, the columns of the great temple tumbled as though a hurricane had blown them down. There are a few steps of broken porticoes, fragments of vanished colonnades, nothing else. This forest of tumbled stones gives off a silvery light, for it is all of Parian marble, the most beautiful of marbles, with a finer grain than the honey-colored Pentelic marble of the Acropolis of Athens. There is something sweet about this stone; it is almost the color of lilies, not white nor silver, but in between; nor does it have the deadness of Carrara but glows inwardly, reflecting as well as absorbing the light, so that when carved into a human shape by a master it seems to breathe. The broken light pours up from the broken stone, but in all this forest there is nowhere where the eye can rest: only the desolation of a great temple, the ruined stumps in the noonday brightness.

Of all the Greek temples this was once the most venerated, for to the Greek imagination the island of Delos was the most sacred of all places. Delphi was nearly as sacred, for there Apollo had established his kingdom on the mainland of Greece, and from there he ruled. But on Delos he was born and spent his youth and first demonstrated his powers. In Delphi he shared his rule with Dionysus; on Delos he was supreme.

Again and again over the years I have returned to the sanctuary of Apollo, haunted by that half-acre of weeds and stone, where the past is buried so that it is almost beyond the power of man to visualize what it must have been. Imagine that all the stones of the Parthenon had tumbled to the ground, and you would be in the same position as the man trying to erect this temple of Apollo in his imagination.

Still the effort can be made, for the French have dug among the ruins and they have a fair idea of what the temple looked like. There was a massive propylon, as at Athens, and six heavy Doric columns guarded the sanctuary which contained the statue of the god, who returned every spring to spend the summer months on his island. Here, too, was the *keraton,* which housed the altar built by Apollo himself out of the horns of his victims. Before the altar, during the celebrations for his return, men danced a strange dance which resembled the flight of cranes. Here, too, was the treasury which contained all the treasure of the Confederacy of Delos. Here was the concentrated wealth of all the Greek city-states in gold and silver bars, in coin and bronze vases, which were also currency among the Greeks. After the Peloponnesian War broke out, the Samians suggested it would be safer to remove the treasure to Athens. The idea appealed strongly to the Athenians, who sensibly used the money to build the Parthenon and to transform Athens into a city of splendor.

Where now there are thistles, there was once the treasure which Athens stole to build her civilization. But if the wealth of the Confederacy was stolen, a great deal must have been left behind, for Apollo demanded his own rich offerings. Homer, or whoever was the author of the *Pythian Hymn to Apollo,* knew this well, for he emphasizes the wealth of those who came to pay tribute to the god:

> *Thou hast many temples and wooded groves,*
> *And all the cliffs and towering peaks*
> *Of the high mountains, and all sea-flowing rivers*
> *Are dear to thee, Apollo, but thou rejoicest most*
> *In Delos. Long-robed Ionians come*
> *To honor thee with their children and gentle women.*
> *Thou art delighted with boxing and dancing and song.*
> *Whenever a festival is held in thy honor,*
> *A man, seeing the Ionians gathered there,*

Would say they were immortal, untouched by age.
He would remark their grace, and rejoice
At the sight of these men and the women with
beautiful girdles
And their swift ships and great wealth . . .

So we may imagine the sanctuary to be filled with sumptuous adornments, bright with color, rich with jewels and bronzes. There were holy relics: Apollo's silver bow, the necklace of Eriphyle, the tiller of Agamemnon, and the mysterious "first-fruits of the Hyperboreans," a relic so holy that after it had been carried solemnly from the land of the Hyperboreans to the Arimaspians, who gave it to the Issedonians, who gave it to the Scythians, who conveyed it to the Greeks in Sinope, who carried it to Prasiae, where the Athenians took possession of it—Pausanias records the adventures of the relic as though he were reading from an inscription in the sanctuary—then at last with proper ceremony it was placed on the sacred ship which left Athens once a year for Delos. What were the "first-fruits of the Hyperboreans"? No one knows. Pausanias says "they were wrapped in wheaten straw, and nobody has any idea what they were."

I confess to a special liking for these first-fruits, so mysterious and invisible. They were among the most sacred treasures of the sanctuary, testifying to the strange winter absences of Apollo in the land of the Hyperboreans which, according to Diodorus Siculus, was Britain. It is pleasant to think of the ancient Britons sending offerings to Delos by way of the one-eyed Arimaspians; and perhaps, after all, the sacred offerings wrapped in wheaten straw were ears of wheat.

Giant Torso

Among the statues crowding the island of Delos there was one which was regarded with a special devotion, because it was already ancient and venerable in classical times, because it was truly colossal, and because many legends were told about it. It dominated all the other statues on the island and stood outside the sanctuary, facing the sea and beckoning the traveler as he sailed through the channel between Delos and Rheneia, a silvery white glittering thing, very noble and beautiful, of which there remain only a foot, a hand, a fragment of the giant torso, another huge fragment of the waist, and the solid base, which has not been moved since the statue was first erected.

The base still stands just outside the sanctuary of Apollo, and still bears the inscription in archaic Greek: "I am the same marble, both statue and base." The base is eleven feet wide, fifteen feet long, and nearly four feet thick, and these figures are important because they suggest the fantastic difficulty of transporting the statue from Naxos, or more probably Paros, where it was carved. The Naxians offered the statue to Apollo's island, probably about 570 B.C. This was their "first-fruit," the most precious offering they could make, and they quite deliberately gave it a commanding position on the shore. It was a time when Naxos was the most powerful island in the Cyclades, dominating the other islands and having Delos under her protection. The statue was therefore more than an offering; it represented the pride of the Naxians in their conquests.

We know the general appearance of the statue, because it is

stamped on an Athenian tetradrachm made about 150 B.C., when it was still standing. Apollo stood naked, in towering majesty, holding in one hand a bow, in the other a kind of plate bearing the images of the three Graces, Euphrosyne who presided over song, Thalia who presided over dancing, and Aglaia who presided over all that was bright and shining in the world. One of the Graces played on her lyre, another on a flute, a third on a shepherd's pipe. Wherever the Graces set up their thrones, Apollo was always present.

One might have thought that Apollo would have been all the more beautiful if he had stood there naked and unadorned, but the Greek imagination delighted in adornments. These Graces were his ornaments. They were his messengers and attendants, but they were also—and this was their most important function—his words. In Delphi he spoke to the world through the lips of the Pythian goddess who dwelt over a chasm leading to the underworld. On Delos he spoke through the Graces, in the sunlight, and there were no chasms leading to the underworld, for here he had no need of them.

His statue stood there for about a hundred and fifty years. In 418 B.C. the Greek general Nicias, during a pause in the Peloponnesian War, decided to place order and regimentation at the service of the god. It occurred to him that the happy, motley crowds who came to worship Apollo, disembarking from their ships in no particular order, throwing garlands hurriedly round their necks and changing their clothes as they disembarked, confusedly singing snatches of hymns as they dragged the sacrificial victims to the altar, these people were doing a disservice to the god, who liked order and the punctilious observation of ritual. Nicias was a millionaire, the owner of silver mines in Attica, a vain, shallow-minded man who was quite properly murdered by the Sicilians a few years later. He decided to build a bridge across the channel between Delos and Rheneia, and the worshippers, suitably attired, would simply march over the bridge and make their offerings to Apollo without for a single moment falling out of line. The bridge was a magnificently gilded affair, hung with tapestries and garlands, with brightly colored railings, especially constructed at Athens at his orders. Along this bridge the worshippers would march in a direct line to the statue of Apollo.

What Nicias really wanted was to secure the special blessing of Apollo. He was prepared to pay for this privilege, and in fact he bought a parcel of land on Delos, at a cost of ten thousand drachmas, for the erection of a temple to Apollo where the priests would continually invoke the god's blessing on Nicias. In the spring of 418 B.C. the orderly procession with Nicias at the head marched across the bridge, the proper offerings were made at the proper time, all the sacrifices were exactly calculated, and the feasts were laid out according to a carefully worked out ritual. Regimentation triumphed, and Nicias regarded himself as the favorite of the god. Apollo, who abhorred straight lines, seems to have felt that Nicias was presuming on a divine friendship, for five years later, when captured by the Syracusans, the god showed not the slightest sign of mercy to the general, who was stabbed to death by his guards, his mangled body thrown outside the city gate as a warning to others.

To the Greeks pride was the gravest of sins, and in his adventurous life Nicias committed many sins of pride. One of them was the gift of a giant bronze tree which he planted beside the statue of the god. Palms were sacred to Apollo, for his mother Leto had clung to a palm tree when she gave birth to her divine child, and there was always a sacred palm tree beside his altar. Odysseus remembered a palm tree at Delos, for when he encountered Nausicaä playing ball, he declared: "I never saw anyone so beautiful, neither man nor woman, and I can only compare you with the young palm tree which I saw when I was at Delos growing near the altar of Apollo."

By removing a real palm tree and placing his own monumental bronze tree beside the statue of Apollo, Nicias committed the sin of pride. His tree was a monument to himself, not to Apollo. During a storm it fell over, crashed against the statue of Apollo, and hurled it to the ground. The statue was apparently not damaged too seriously, for it was put back in place. Nothing more was ever heard of the bronze tree.

For a few more years the statue welcomed travelers to the holy island, and then it vanishes from history. We hear of it again in the early years of the fifteenth century when the Florentine traveler Buondelmonte visited Delos. He gives a tantalizingly brief description of it. He made plans to carve up the statue, in order to transport it to Florence, but after some halfhearted attempts to carve up the base he thought better of the enterprise. Two centuries later, in the reign of King Charles I, Sir Kenelm Digby, poet and traveler, visited the island and paid particular attention to the sanctuary of Apollo. He tells us that the statue was still lying there, broken in two pieces about the waist, and he adds that though many had tried to carry it away they had all failed.

Other visitors came, and all caught a glimpse of it. A Netherlander of the seventeenth century described it as a statue of Artemis, perhaps because of the thick curls which fall down Apollo's back, and the same mistake was made by Thevenot in 1655. In

1673 the painter Seger de Vries found no sign of the legs, but the head was still in existence, for he made an astonishing surrealistic sketch of the island, showing Mount Cynthus in the background, with the colossal bust of the Naxian Apollo standing among the columns, with a huge fragment of the torso lying some distance away. Three years later the head had vanished, for Sir George Wheler wrote that Apollo was "so entirely ruined that it is impossible to judge as to its form, and the God himself so ill-handled that he had neither hands, feet, nor head left him, yet what is remaining appeareth still more beautiful; his locks hanging around his shoulders are yet to be seen, having marked on each curl (as we judge) where Jewels had been set, with a sign about the waist of a girdle, which had in like manner been richly adorned, and on his left shoulder a light mantle. The statue was about four or five times bigger than Nature, and no less than a Colossus, for the shoulders were six feet broad."

Sir George Wheler was a man with an unusual understanding of Greek sculpture, and when he spoke of the places where jewels had been set, he was speaking of the holes drilled into the marble to support long vanished ribbons of gold. As for the light mantle on the left shoulder of Apollo, this seems to have been the product of his imagination. The god was never clothed.

By the early eighteenth century the processes of corruption and disfigurement had advanced to such a state that there remained only the two colossal fragments which remain today. Tournefort writes sadly of the broken hulk of the god, of which there remained only two pieces, "the Back for one, the Belly and the Thighs for the other; they have left him neither Head, nor Arms, nor Legs. It was a colossal Statue of a single Block of Marble, the Hair falling about his Shoulders in large rings. The Back is six feet broad, but there are no signs of any ornament to be seen, nor do the oldest inhabitants of *Mycone* remember they ever saw that figure whole; the Trunk of it is quite naked, and is ten foot from the Haunch to the Knee." In Tournefort's day the thighs of Apollo remained, but otherwise he saw what we see today.

Year by year Apollo is melting away. The frosts, the winds, the rains nibble at the once-proud form of the most beautiful and youthful of the gods, and the sun, his servant, scorches him. Yet what remains is strangely moving, for time has provided an abstract portrait of the god with the broad shoulders and the cascading curls. All that was inconsequential and merely human has been smoothed away, leaving only the powerful thrusting shape of divinity.

Myconos

THE ANCIENT GREEKS never had a good word for Myconos. It was an island almost without history and without legends. Poseidon or Hercules—no one was quite sure which—had hurled that rock at the Giants and forever buried them beneath the sea, and that was all they could tell you about the island in antiquity. The rock was useful only for filling the Giants' grave.

Although Myconos lies close to Delos, Apollo never paid any attention to the island, no ruined temples have ever been found, and the museum is littered with ancient vases from all the surrounding islands, but there are none from Myconos. Just as Delos was the holy island, so Myconos became the cursed island, the island of the grave-fill, with its bad harbor and dangerous currents and bleak uninteresting hills where nothing seems to grow except some ragged vines. There are people on the island who say they have never seen a tree, but they are exaggerating. There are in fact a few stunted trees, gnarled and bent by the *meltemi,* the violent northwest wind which threatens to blow everything away; the locations of the trees are known, and it is said that a town councillor has been given the special duty of watching over and preserving them, while another town councillor has been placed in charge of the 364 churches on the island to see that those which are washed away in the storms are immediately replaced. Some of these churches are not much larger than dog kennels, while the largest is the size of an ordinary house. They are family churches, erected by frightened sailors to honor vows made during tempests; they are testimonies to the storms of the Cyclades rather than to the sanctity of the Myconiots. The islanders are proud of their 364 churches, which works out at one for every ten inhabitants.

Strabo offers the curious information that the Myconiots went bald at the age of twenty or twenty-five, but provided no explanation for this strange phenomenon. Pliny notes that the children of the islanders were always born without hair. It was as though the poverty of the island extended even to hair. Poverty, indeed, was the ever-present companion of Myconos. Archilochus, the poet, reproached a certain Pericles for coming to a feast "like a Myconiot," meaning that he had come uninvited. It became a proverb. Ovid wrote of "humble Myconos," meaning perhaps that it was dull and poor and not worth any man's attention.

But times have changed, and the grave-fill island is no longer unworthy of attention. It has no history, and nothing ever happens there except that the tourists come and go, and at least once a year the waves break down the sea-wall. Precisely because it has no history the island acquires a character of charming irrelevance. There is no need to do anything on Myconos. There are no dates to be learned and remembered, no gods to be propitiated except perhaps Dionysus whose emblem, together with a bunch of grapes, appears incomprehensibly on its ancient coins. Outside time, outside history, Myconos sleeps its long sleep like the dead Giants who lie below.

It is an island I have always returned to with pleasure, but never with any desire to stay very long. The beauty of the town lies in its white houses overlooking the crescent-shaped harbor, and the narrow whitewashed streets where even the donkeys tread delicately to avoid staining the purity of the place. It is a very ordinary and commonplace whitewash, but since the houses are arranged in tiers along the hillside, perspective and distance lend subtle variations to whiteness. There are grey whites, pearly whites, pink whites, even purple whites. There are the gleaming whites of eyeballs, and the dry, sinister whites of skeletons, and all these whites are colored by the blue heavens. To wander through those luminous lanes is to experience white in so many multitudinous forms that you wonder whether you have ever seen white before.

The small white village climbing the hills is quite formless. There is no center, no main square, nothing except the rococo church of the Paraportiani on the seashore to attract attention. Paraportiani means "through the gates," and no doubt there was a sea-gate here long ago. The church has the effect of breaking the monotony of the square cubes of houses by an admirable use of curved vaults, cupolas and belfries. The winds have melted the stepped walls into curves, and indeed the whole building gives the impression of a Christmas cake melting in the summer heat, soon to become no more than a lake of icing. Yet to compare it with a Christmas cake is to mistake its soaring unity of form, the outriding buttresses supporting one another, the belfry echoing the shape of the cupola and both being echoed by the dome over the entrance of one of the four chapels, all at different levels and corresponding to the four points of the compass. The architect, faced with an almost insoluble problem, succeeded in his abstract design almost too brilliantly. It is a small church, and you have to bend your head to enter the low doorways, but the architect has given it the magnitude of a fortress.

On a summer's day the white church resembles a painted backcloth, flat and unanchored against the fiery sky, which is only a little less bright than the sky over Delos. But storms come quickly in the Cyclades, and after we had been wandering for half an hour through the blazing whiteness of the streets, we came out at last into the little rubble-strewn square to find the church suddenly grey with shadow. A storm had come up in the twinkling of an eye, grey clouds were shooting low over the sea, and you could hear the waves slapping against the sea-wall and the shouts of the fishermen. In this light Alexander photographed the church, giving to it the solemnity and beauty it deserved. From being a plaything it became a monument.

Inside the Paraportiani is intolerably drab with nineteenth century icons. An old woman hovered there, scarcely distinguishable from the shadows thrown on the walls of those four narrow chambers, which might have been tombs. She was ninety-four years old, and spent her life going from one chapel to another to pray for the souls of the dead; and it seemed to please her that there were few visitors and that the dead were many.

When we came out of the Paraportiani the brief summer storm was over and the sun was shining again. As usual, there were hordes of visitors on the quay, many of them grouped around the famous pelican called Petros, who has become the emblem of Myconos, as the owl was the emblem of Athens. Every time I have come to Myconos, I have found Petros standing in the same place, somnolent, ill-kempt, and gorged with fish. He rarely moves. He stands guard. He is horrible.

But when the sun is shining, it is the purest pleasure to sit in one of the cafés overlooking the bay, watching the caïques sailing in and out, for the big ships anchor offshore, not daring to enter the inner harbor. There is a ceaseless hubbub. A three-year-old boy rides by on a donkey with the air of a young prince. A German marches along the quay in *lederhosen* with the air of a conqueror. Girls run about in blue jeans. Americans from the Midwest plod after their wives. Alas, the wives have bought the flamboyant skirts which are one of the specialities of Myconos, and these skirts have the effect of making broad beams broader. Their menfolk clutch cameras, smoke cigars and wear carnations behind their ears; they suffer their wives in silence. Swedes blow conches, and the English wear beards. A Myconiot caïque-owner appears out of nowhere and offers to take you to Naxos for the same price he paid for his caïque. But soon enough the three-year-old prince on his donkey returns to scatter the vision of Vanity Fair. He wears his shapeless rags with so great an air of defiance and rides so purposefully that you imagine he is a visitor from another age, pleased to watch the caprices of the present.

The quay-side cafés form a small enclosed world of their own. They seem to have nothing to do with the enchanted white village which lies behind them; the waiters might have stepped out of the Deux Magots in Paris. Twenty languages are being spoken, everyone is running about madly, and only the waiters remain calm. The pleasure lies in watching the seething activity on the quay-side and in the harbor filled with its overladen boats.

Years ago, when I first visited Myconos, I was struck by an astonishing relief in the museum gardens. It was quite small, and showed a youth lying prone on the earth, and over him were the words: *Ego dormio et cor meum vigilat.* I sleep and my heart keeps watch. Though the words were in Latin, such brevity and quiet grief seemed peculiarly Greek. There was no name, no date, nothing to suggest the origin of this stone carving which may go back to the time of the Crusaders. It was a haunting sentence, and the anonymous youth was also haunting. Since those days I have learned a little bit more about the carving. I have learned that Alexander Drummond, visiting Myconos about 1750, found nothing to interest him in the island "unless you have in mind to admire an inscription on a tombstone reading as follows: *Ego dormio et cor meum vigilat.*" So he wrote in his book *Travels through different parts of Germany and Asia* which appeared in 1754. It was the only object on the island which he found in the least tolerable.

Today the carving is no longer in the museum garden. A new folklore museum has been erected near the Paraportiani, with a wonderful hodgepodge of ancient books, maps, keys, candlesticks, and engravings, and the boy who sleeps and keeps watch shares one of the rooms with an engraving of the battle of Navarino and another of Kaiser Wilhelm II. Evidently there has been a division of spoils. The museum takes ancient Greece, leaving everything that is not ancient Greece to the folklorists. It seems a pity, for the sleeping youth was in good company among the ancient marbles in the enchanted garden of the museum.

The garden has not changed; only the youth has been removed.

°

The headless statues still lean against the wall under the shade of the trees; one day the fruit will fall, and the figures in their stiff draperies will be headless no longer. It is a secluded garden, far from the wild traffic of the quay-side. Here the empty tombs of Greeks, Romans, Franks, Venetians and Turks lie in happy confusion, all history jumbled together. Far away across the harbor lie the red and blue domes, and the white houses, and the whitewashed latticed dovecotes on the hills. At such times Myconos comes into its own, and you can forget Petros and all the other pelicans gorging themselves with fish.

Naxos

WE CAME to Naxia, the capital of the island of Naxos, by island steamer, seeing only the faint glimmer of the white city in the starlight. It was very dark. There was the smell of lemons and dried blood, of night dews and of damp seeping through ancient walls. A lame youth with a long mottled neck and heavily lidded eyes emerged from the crowd at the foot of the swaying gangway and seized our luggage. Limping heavily he led us up through streets of whitewashed stairways, through a labyrinth of narrow alleyways, to a remote hotel which had the strange empty purposeless look of a provincial police station. Pale from the long climb, he began to tell us that he was a student at the University of Athens, but his mother had fallen ill and he was forced to return to the island, where he had no future, no hope of advancement. "With my education, what future do I have?" he asked, and we would have been more sympathetic if we had not felt that he had told the story before to many midnight visitors. Getting rid of him was difficult. Limping about the empty hotel, he offered to be our guide, swore eternal affection, described his mother's many illnesses, offered us travel folders and postcards, and finally explained that the hotelkeeper was paying him nothing for finding us a hotel so late at night, and it was up to us whether we should reward him for his services. Decidedly Naxos left a bad first impression. Those dark and labyrinthine streets, the smell of dried blood, the lame youth seemed to have escaped out of a nightmare. The sea-mist was coming in, and from the balcony the whole city seemed to have been lightly powdered with frost.

Robert Liddell, the *doyen* of Aegean travelers, found nothing to please him in Naxia. He called it "filthy" and "tumble-down," and said of the walls that "they hopefully ask you not to throw rubbish on them." He was glad to leave the island for nearby Paros, which was more civilized and altogether more conventional. Naxia has no churches worth mentioning, while Paros has the beautiful and romantic church of Our Lady of a Hundred Gates, said to have been founded by St. Helena on the spot where she had the vision of the Cross. And then, too, Naxia is curiously closed in, huddled on its rock like white flies on a dungheap, while Paros wanders happily along a green waterfront. Still, I prefer Naxia. It is dirty, but no dirtier than most of the other towns on the Greek islands. It is cleaner than Chios. The lavatories work. The few shops are well stocked, and the people are red-cheeked and healthy. The upper town, consisting of the small whitewashed palaces of descendants of the Venetian nobility still bearing their carved patents of nobility over the doorways, is oddly colorless and tiresome. The smell of blood is all-pervading; every butcher's shop reeked of skinned and disemboweled goats; but this may mean only that Naxos eats better than the other islands.

One could draw up a good-sized list of particulars: the streets so cavernous, the wine so acid, the famous liqueur made from lemons so sour, and the town so empty of interest. Then beside this list one must draw up another, for there are many admirable things to be found in Naxos. It has the best museum of Cycladic art in the world. There is a charming white church set on a minuscule island offshore. The town is admirably designed to be seen from the sea, resembling a pyramid of cascading children's toys. There are sandy beaches. Half a mile from the town you are among soaring hills which have the same grandeur as the mountains of Chios. Some eight or nine miles away, in a village garden, there is an extraordinary sculpture of a kouros carved from the living marble and left uncompleted. There are sweet-water wells which almost taste of wine. There are flowers in abundance. Above all there is the gate of Apollo, and that single gate standing alone on its island is worth all the trouble of the journey. Creamy yellow, glinting with gold lights, small and yet massive, beautiful in all its dimensions, the marble gate speaks with an ultimate authority. Here at last you come face to face with Apollo.

The Gate of Apollo

Again and again as you travel among the Greek islands you see the footsteps of Apollo. The young god with the silver bow and the yellow flowing hair is still present in the air; he still hurtles through the skies; he still hovers over the tongues of poets and the chisels of sculptors, demanding an always impossible perfection. There is nothing mild in him, for he is the god of power, of sudden death and of relentless vengeance, who heals as quietly as he kills. Youthful, never dying, he is the god of the divine energy.

So it will happen that when you are walking alone along a forest pathway overlooking the sea, there will be a sudden inexplicable shining as the god announces his presence, and any peasant will tell you it is the shining of his hair in the sun, or a smile, or simply an annunciation. He comes when least expected. Indeed his landfalls and departures are always "least expected," for he is usually far away, a remote and curiously august personage who rarely appears to men, and then only very casually, when he is unbidden, or at moments of intense crisis. The ancients knew him well, and we, who sometimes pretend that he no longer possesses an empire over men's minds, even now acknowledge his empire over the arts.

The Naxians knew him well, and were among his first worshippers. They took Delos under their protection, and represented themselves as protectors and guardians of the shrine. Under the tyrant Lygdamis, the contemporary of the Athenian Peisistratus, they ruled the Aegean in alliance with Athens, and it was during this period that there occurred the famous transfer of the dead from Delos to Rheneia. For Peisistratus it was intolerable that death should touch the island of the god of divine purity, and so for centuries no one was permitted to die or be buried on Delos.

Naxos grew to wealth and power, faithful to Apollo. At Apollona in the north of the island, there can still be seen in the marble quarry an unfinished statue of Apollo thirty-four feet long, lying in its marble bed. It is rough-hewn, not yet recognizably a portrait of a god, but impressive by reason of its vast size. It looks, in fact, like a curiously carved white marble tree-trunk: elsewhere on the island are other carvings still lying in the quarries, abandoned by the sculptors for unknown causes. Earthquakes, pirate raids, plagues— we can only guess.

In the town of Naxos itself, on a little spit of gorse-covered land jutting out to sea, there stands a marble gateway so beautiful, of such perfect proportions, that it acquires almost the appearance of a portrait of the god, in the same way that the Parthenon is an abstract portrait of Athene. The marble, once silvery white, has grown creamy yellow with age. This gateway is all that remains of the small temple of Apollo that once stood on this headland. Half-moons of columns lie nearby, and there are traces of a stairway and a marble pathway. It stands there with superb authority, not very large or imposing, being some twenty feet high and twelve feet broad, and with no decoration except the bosses for supporting the heavy wooden doors, which have long since vanished. There are only the plain uprights and the crossbeam against the perfect blue skies of the Aegean, and you wonder whether there is any other place in the Cyclades where there is such perfection, such serenity.

This gateway seems to open out on splendid entertainments and solemn adventures.

It is never mentioned in history, and there are no inscriptions. It seems to have been there since the beginning of time, to have grown out of the headland and to have become a part of it. But in fact it is possible to make a reasonable guess at its origins. The proportions suggest a date about 550 B.C., which would make it contemporary with Lygdamis, the tyrant of Naxos, who reigned at a time when the Naxians controlled the seaways of the Cyclades. It was the gift of the Naxians to Apollo. They set the temple on the headland so that they could receive Apollo's blessing, as their ships set sail for the mysterious island of Delos in the north.

It must have been a very small temple, scarcely larger than the temple to Athene Nike on the Acropolis, with four columns in the front and back, and a processional way. No doubt the roof was of marble tiles, for the Naxians claimed to be the first to roof buildings with tiles, and perhaps there was a frieze describing the adventures and wanderings of Apollo. Today the headland is an island reached by a causeway, and in those ancient days it was probably reached by boats from the mainland, and in these boats they would bring the white oxen for sacrifice. The island was another Delos, sacred to Apollo. Within the temple there would be the cult statue of the god, naked, holding his silver bow in one hand and perhaps the three Graces in the other. When the doors were flung open, Apollo would smile and gaze out to sea toward the island where he was born and where he had his home.

Then the choristers would come and sing the praises of the god who was their sovereign, and they would dance and sacrifice the oxen and play on their golden lyres:

> *O golden lyre, shared by Apollo with the Muses,*
> *The violet-haired: the dancers and the choristers heed you,*
> *And the singers obey your measures when,*
> *Shaken by the music, you set the beat for the dance.*
> *You have the power to quench the flaming bolt*
> *Of heavenly fire. On the sceptre of Zeus*
> *The Eagle sleeps, having folded his quick wings,*
> *O King of Birds!*
> *You have shed a dark mist on his drooping head,*

Royal stairway at Phaistos.

Temple of Athena Lindia from the sea.

Fortress on the mole, Rhodes.

Statue of Isis in a field, Gortyn.

The Lion of Venice at Rhodes.

Turkish cemetery at Rhodes.

Windmills on the jetty at Rhodes.

The grave of Nikos Kazantzakis at Heracleion.

His eyelids are closed with a sweet seal,
He dreams, and his lithe back ripples
In the quivering spell of your song. The war god,
The fierce one, putting aside his harsh pride
Of spears, also succumbs to sleep.
The arrows of music soothe the heart of the gods
By virtue of the wisdom of Apollo and the deep-girdled Muses.

So Pindar sings, extolling the power and wisdom of Apollo over all the other gods, even the most wise and the most powerful. Through music Apollo reigns over all.

For more than a thousand years the gate of Apollo vanished. The temple became a Christian church under the Byzantines and the Venetians; it became a mosque when Naxos fell to the Turks. At last in 1926 the archaeologists tore down the ruined walls of the mosque and revealed the gate in all its purity.

That day when we climbed up the narrow pathway, we were dazzled by the midday glare. There were no clouds in the shattering blue of the heavens. The small, low-lying island is only two hundred yards from the town, but once you have crossed the causeway you are in another world. The yellow gorse was in bloom. Grey lizards darted among the broken columns and the marble pebbles. The indigo-blue sea murmured with a soft lapping, and there was only the stillness of the small island.

At first when you see the gateway you are struck by the richness of the marble, its lightness, the way it balances easily on the highest point of the island, the wonderful simplicity of the design. It wears an air of permanence with casual grace. Afterward you realize that its simplicity is a delusion, that it is a remarkably complex structure with its bosses and sockets and time-worn grooves, and that it is superbly functional. Simplicity vanishes in its many surfaces. One has the feeling that the gateway has been set up, and the architects and masons are nearby and soon the rest of the temple will be built. What we are seeing is not the ruin of a temple, but its first beginnings.

I confess I could never quite bring myself to believe in the power of Apollo until I came to Naxos. There are few good portraits of Apollo; the best of them appear on Sicilian coins where he is represented as a youth of extraordinary beauty, with something menacing in the pure refinement of his features. These portraits are clearly based on young aristocrats of grave sweetness and sensibility; they only hint at the face of the god. He is not to be found in the ruins of Delos and Delphi, those forests of stone drums and overturned columns, the broken bones of the god spread over acres and acres of land. The two *Homeric Hymns to Apollo* and Pindar's *Odes* present him vividly, and on rare occasions he appears in Greek tragedy, but always as a remote and mysterious figure, a kind of shining in the air. Here he comes down to earth. His features, his smile, his sense of order, his springing limbs are all suggested in the gateway. Here on this island he lives in marble.

Today the Naxians call the gateway the *palatia,* the palace, a word they inherited from the Venetians. It is Apollo's palace, one of the few that remain.

The Kouros

We drove out of Naxia on one of those high wide days when the clouds seem to be skimming across a blue marble sky. The winding road among the lemon groves was white with summer dust, and the air was succulent with the promise of fruit. Not that there was any great wealth on the island; we saw no other cars on the roads; the few villages are widely scattered, and the people poor. Once the island was famous for its lemons, which were exported all over the world, but now there are only a few markets left for them. The vineyards too were famous, but no one any longer speaks with any great respect of Naxian wine.

There was a feeling of emptiness and desolation, so few were the people, so rare the villages. The hills were pleasantly ferocious, the roads were bad. Once more we heard the familiar complaint of the driver that Athens took the island's taxes and gave nothing in return; certainly Athens was doing nothing about providing good roads. Here and there we came upon a stone-cutter or a peasant working in the fields, but the landscape seemed deserted, forgotten, dying in the sun.

The road became worse, and we marveled at the driver who seemed to delight in tearing his car to pieces on the rocks. Suddenly he swerved into a narrow side road even more dangerous, no more than a scratched-out path of boulders, and over this we lurched toward a patch of intense green. There were flowerbeds and vegetable gardens at the bottom of the valley, and we learned that they were watered by a famous well, which was very ancient.

"It is the sweetest water in Naxos," the driver said, and smiled happily, for we were already covered with the choking white dust from the road.

The well was a great cavern, reached by steps, dark and silvery, and you could hear the thunder of the water against the walls. How old the well was we never learned, and the driver could only tell us that it had been there as long as he could remember, which was some twenty-five years. It may have been there for as many centuries.

So we splashed our faces in the sweet water, nearly ice-cold, and drank it in cupped hands, and forgot the kouros we had come to see, until the driver reminded us that it was only a little way along the road in a small walled garden.

A kouros is a ceremonial statue of a naked youth, usually standing with his hands by his side and his left foot forward. They were carved in the sixth century B.C. as offerings to the gods, or as memorials to athletes who won victories at the games, or as memorials to the dead. They could be of any size, but were more often life-size. Among the Kouroi are some of the supreme achievements of Greek art.

The kouros in the small garden lay on his back, brown and mottled with age, his legs broken at the ankle. Nearby was the marble rock from which he had been carved. His arms were still joined to his sides, his legs clung together, and his head was shaped like an egg. Yet he was undeniably powerful as he lay there, with his huge chest and powerful shoulders. It was quiet in the garden. A village girl came and dangled her legs over the wall, smiling in the dappled sunlight. The fig trees offered a little shade, and there were lilies in the gardens all round.

"Please notice," said the driver, "that the kouros has lost his genitals. It is not his fault. An American lady came here some years ago and she chopped them off with a chisel. It is terrible what some American ladies can do."

When we left the garden he was still shaking his head sadly.

The Old Professor

He was an old man, worn to the bone, and there was something about his manner and his voice which suggested that he took comfort from his years and had lived very fully in many capitals and known many adventures. He was nearly eighty years old. His skin was burned by the sun, and his dark eyes under the beetling brows gleamed with hidden amusement. They said of him that he very rarely permitted visitors to enter his museum, and was irascible when they failed to appreciate the treasures he had accumulated, and would sometimes send them packing if he thought they were unworthy. They said he had a terrible rage. We found him gentle and mild. It was one of those terribly hot days when the air is like a sheet of flame, but he wore a thick black woolen suit, with a gaily colored scarf round his neck.

"So you have come to see my collection of toys," he said, smiling on the steps of the museum and dangling a six-inch key. "Well, it is a good day for seeing them."

He did not explain why this day was better than any other day, but he seemed pleased that we had come, as though he had been expecting us for a long time. He spoke in French, without an accent, and wore a black wide-brimmed hat which gave him something of the appearance of a French scholar. His name, he told us, was Nikolaos Gavalas. It was a good name. In the Middle Ages a Leo Gavalas had proclaimed himself Despot of Rhodes, Caesar and Master of the Cyclades, and struck his own coins.

Though frail, the old man climbed quickly up the steps, put the key in the lock, and gave it a quick turn. Then he slipped inside and vanished in the shadows, while we accustomed ourselves to living in this darkness, no longer in the sun's glare.

It was a very small museum, white and blue, the two rooms lit by small windows. There was grey dust on the marble floor, for it was rarely visited, and sometimes through the corners of our eyes we would see Dr. Gavalas surreptitiously sweeping the dust away with a straw broom, as though he felt it was beneath the dignity of the museum that there should be a speck of dust anywhere. He was always a mysterious gaunt figure who seemed to appear and disappear as he pleased.

There were the usual Venetian lions, urns, and headless statues of Hellenistic boys. There were stone capitals with Corinthian volutes and the inevitable anthemia with curling petals, but it was not for these that the museum had acquired its fame. In some eight or nine glass cases were the doctor's "toys," rarely more than three inches high, all carved out of marble and most of them representing a woman in the attitude of perfect repose, arms folded across her breast, face tilted back, no eyes, no mouth, sharp triangular nose. They are called Cycladic figures, and there were more than fifty of them in the room. It was in fact the world's largest collection of these rare figures which are worth far more than their weight in gold.

Today, without mouths or eyes, these figures have the look of abstractions of the human form, but this is not how they appeared when they were carved. Originally they were painted; there were blue rings for eyes, and red on the lips, and they were clothed with paint, and wore painted hair and necklaces. Now like the Parthenon, they have been stripped of ornament, reduced almost to skeletons of themselves, being ghosts of the brightly colored dolls who once inhabited the Bronze Age graves, protecting the dead. For the most part they were goddesses of fertility, small breasted and thick waisted, with the look of youth. Usually they were placed face upward in the grave, and they can scarcely have represented anything else but the hope of resurrection. Not all were small: some have been found three feet high or more; and not all were goddesses, for a few indisputably male gods have been found, and they too have their arms folded across their chests and their heads are tilted back a little. Strangely, those tip-tilted heads possess an extraordinary resemblance to the heads in Modigliani's paintings with their pointed noses and faintly sketched eyes and mouths. These Cycladic figures, unknown until the present century, buried in the earth for five thousand years, are completely modern in feeling. They seem to have come to the surface at exactly the right time.

So we gazed at them, while Dr. Gavalas swept the floor with his straw broom, and from time to time he would indicate some special delicacy of form in those figures. They were like drops of ice preserved over fifty centuries, and somewhere embedded in them were the secrets of a way of life now altogether forgotten. What was enviable was the perfect serenity of these figures, the calm expectation written on those features, which were not features, but abstract delineations of godlike form.

"Ce sont des petits jouets," Dr. Gavalas said, and his heavily lidded eyes lit up with secret amusement, for he knew better and was pleased with us for being reverent in their presence.

And then he began to talk about how the archaeologists had dug up these specks of glinting marble, usually on a hillside facing the west, but sometimes by the seashore, and in fact there was no telling where they might appear, for the Bronze Age islanders buried their dead all over the islands. He pointed to a kingly figure with a conical cap, also of marble, one of the rarest of Cycladic figures, and he said gently: "Look, it is the beginning of sculpture." And it was so. There was the faintest of expressions on the face, the arms and legs were more articulated, there was the sense of muscular power. In time this figure would grow and become the eager, three-dimensional Apollo of the classical age, life-size and dominating everything around it, but here, in its beginnings, it was still very small and frail.

It pleased Dr. Gavalas that Christian Zervos, the great authority on Cycladic art, had written his monumental works before he had seen the museum at Naxos.

"I could have told him a thing or two," he chuckled. "Why, he saw these little marble figures all over the world, he had been to all the museums, but it never occurred to him that in Naxos we have our own collection. And how delighted he was! He came here and poured out his heart to them and apologized most deeply for the oversight. I could not take him away from them."

He went on chuckling to himself, and then he said: "We found the skeletons lying on their sides, and the figures lay about where their stomachs would have been. Beads, too, and many trinkets, and little boxes where the women kept the paint for their cheeks and eyelids."

He went on to speak of a silvered spearhead and three small golden lions, not much larger than a thumb, evidently of Mycenaean workmanship, found recently by the hotelkeeper Michael Zeycolis. They were reddish gold, and may have decorated a royal throne.

Later we saw the Cycladic figures in the museum at Paros. There are fifty in Naxos, Paros has only sixteen. These sixteen are heavier and cruder, with longer necks; they resemble rough copies of Naxian originals. It was a small museum near the church of Our Lady of a Hundred Gates, chiefly remarkable for the statue of a girl whose enchanting body is clothed in a peplos of worn russet marble. The kindly museum director at Paros gave us flowers as we left. Dr. Gavalas, with the same exquisite courtesy, asked us whether we had enjoyed his "little toys" and bowed us down the steps.

Filthy Naxos? Perhaps. But what other island has row upon row of brilliant Cycladic figures, a marble kouros lying in a stone-walled garden, and the face of Apollo at the sunlit gate?

Tinos

THEY TELL the story of a ship's captain who spent many years in the Orient and when he returned at last to Tinos he found the spell of the Orient still so strong that he built himself a Chinese house and imported Chinese servants and even went to the length of taking a Chinese concubine, and every day he would go down to the harbor in the hope of finding some sailor with the latest news of Shanghai or Macao. The years passed. Few sailors brought him the news he wanted to hear. He promised himself he would make one last journey to the Orient, but he was already old. Then he said: "If I cannot go to the East, then the East must come to me," and he decided to transform Tinos into an oriental town. He began by putting up Chinese lanterns all round the harbor, and he would have gone on to put flaring roofs and yellow tiles on all the houses, but died before he could put the plan into effect. He was, however, given a Chinese funeral, and somewhere in the hills there is said to be his tomb, facing east and surmounted by a stone elephant.

The story may not be true, but there is no doubt that the harbor is ringed with Chinese lanterns. It is a pleasant harbor, quite small, with the inevitable promenade where the couples walk under the lanterns every evening. Great blocks of marble lie about the harbor, waiting to be shipped to Athens. But it is not for its exports of marble, or even for the Chinese lanterns on the waterfront, that Tinos is famous among the Greeks. Its fame derives from the white church of Panayia Evangelistria, where twice a year pilgrims from all over Greece come to offer their prayers and to hope for miraculous cures.

Almost Tinos is an island without history. Like Myconos, it seems to have been sparsely populated in classical times. It was a harsh and rugged island, never very rich. Tinos is said to derive from a Phoenician word meaning "snake," and it is certain that the islanders once prayed to Poseidon the Snake-killer rather than Poseidon, god of the sea. The Venetians conquered the island and built an inland capital which they called Borgo; it is a pirate's lair on top of a mountain. There is a nunnery where the saintly Pelagaya in old age had visions of Jesus; her bare cell, her knife and fork, her bed and skull are piously preserved. There are huge marble dovecotes, more harshly decorative even than those at Myconos. There are the ruins of a temple of Poseidon, and a small and well-kept museum where the most notable object on display is a red vase six feet high with some wonderful archaic reliefs. But inevitably you find yourself returning to the Panayia Evangelistria, the white church reached by a marble street overlooking the bay.

A Wonder-Working Icon

One day in 1822 some workmen digging in the hill above the small port of Tinos struck their spades against wood. At first they thought they had struck the roots of a tree and this annoyed them, for they were digging a well. Then they saw a blue and ghostly flame rising from the earth, and they made out the shapes of a painting on wood. A priest was summoned. Within an hour they had unearthed a holy icon painted by St. Luke showing the Angel of the Annunciation in the presence of the Virgin. The spade had cut the icon in two.

Such is the story told about the wonder-working icon of the Panayia, and they add that the icon was well known in the Middle Ages and venerated with as much fervor as it is venerated today. There are documents attesting to its antiquity and to its secret burial during the time of the Turkish invasions. There are also documents written by the workmen who discovered it; all of them had seen the blue flame.

The blue flame! It is always there, whenever some mysterious and beautiful object is recovered from the earth; so the priests say, and the peasants, who are as wise as priests, will tell you they see the flame at night hovering over their fields. The blue flame, announcing the presence of hidden treasures, haunts the Greek imagination. For the Greeks the surface to the earth is beautiful, but there is a still greater beauty below the earth. The legend of the earth mother Demeter still flourishes; even now she wanders in search of her lost daughter, the golden-haired Persephone, who lies buried beneath the earth, coming to birth in the spring. For the Greeks mysterious veins of holiness lie in the rocks; there are hoards of jewels beneath all the floorboards. They are a people who have buried their treasures for so many centuries that they are accustomed to regarding the earth as a treasure-chest.

So the wonder-working icon came to light, and at first it attracted little attention. A small chapel was built for it. It was encased in a golden frame, and contemporary artists copied it. From these copies it would appear to be a Byzantine work of the early thirteenth century, with intricate designs of canopies and terraces, and an immensely elongated Gabriel hovering beside the Virgin. Gradually its fame increased. The chapel became a church, and pilgrims came twice a year on the two great feasts of Our Lady, the twenty-fifth of March and the fifteenth of August. The second feast, being the day of the Assumption, attracted the greater number of pilgrims. By the end of the century the icon, which had been buried for centuries, was buried again under a rococo coating of jewels. There is such a thick encrustation of gold, silver, emeralds, diamonds and rubies that the icon has been wholly submerged except for two small pear-shaped openings for the face of Gabriel and the face of the Virgin. The openings are little pools of darkness, for the painting is so faded that nothing can be seen.

The church grew larger and larger, for the sick and the maimed came in vast numbers to be cured by the wonder-working icon. The *Megalohari,* "the great and gracious Lady" of Tinos, became more famous and more powerful, until she extended her sway over the whole of Greece, becoming at last the protectress of the nation and an emblem of national unity. As the *Tiniotissa* she rules over the destiny of the Greeks, and she is especially devoted to sailors.

On August 15, 1940 the Greek cruiser *Elli* was lying at anchor off the port of Tinos. It was a hot summer day, with hundreds of caïques crowding the harbor. The cruiser was beflagged in honor of the wonder-working Madonna whose feast day it was. The pilgrims, who had come from all over Greece, were making their way up the broad road which leads from the harbor to the church when they heard the explosion. A submarine had sent a torpedo into the side of the *Elli* without warning. It was an Italian submarine, and two months later Italy declared war on Greece.

In a strange way the shock of the explosion bound the *Tiniotissa* even more closely to Greek hearts. The dead sailors were offerings on her altar, and it was remembered that in ancient times Tinos belonged to the sea god Poseidon, who also demanded sacrifices. The treachery of the Italians did not dishearten the Greeks, but on the contrary made them more determined and more desperate. The lifebelts of the sunken cruiser were given a special place of honor in the church.

When we reached the church it was midday, with the sun high overhead in a blinding sky. The church resembled a Christmas cake with the icing still being poured on it, so new and so gleaming that it had an unfinished look. The icing poured over the courtyard and onto an ornate marble fountain. Palm trees flanked the marble stairways. Without too much difficulty one could imagine that the church was built yesterday and was the country house of a rich Tiniot shipowner. Decidedly it had no resemblance to the usual Greek church. It was Christmas cake, country mansion, wild improvisation of monumental stairways, balconies and archways. Somewhere nearby a typewriter was clicking away.

The Tiniots have done their best, but they have not succeeded in giving the church an air of sanctity; it wears a festive air. Those stairways are to be climbed on horseback by men with feathers in their caps. In the forecourt you would expect to find a seesaw and children playing. But that morning the approaches to the church were deserted; the typewriter clicked away; the cobbled mosaics in the courtyard were blinding; the icing was still being poured over the white façade.

Nor does the interior of the church resemble anything else to be found in Greece. It looks like a treasure casket. Hundreds of silver and gold lamps, in triple rows, hang from the ceiling. There are crystal chandeliers, candelabras and candlesticks five feet tall. Votive offerings of hammered silver are everywhere. Icons abound, but they too are encased in silver with only the smoke-darkened heads of the saints still visible. Victorian oleographs line the walls, but they can do nothing to deflect the prevailing silvery shimmer which seems to leap continually from one side of the room to the other, filling the room with silver air. On the window ledges heaped rose petals stir in the summer wind; they are dry and crackle a little. The doors are flung wide open. Down below, beyond the blinding forecourt, lies the blue sea.

Here the Virgin reigns quietly and intimately in her silver palace. She is "the great and gracious Lady," but she is also *stella maris,* the star of the sea, her powers reaching as far as the seas reach. At first sight her holy wonder-working icon looks as though it has been dredged from the sea and is still encrusted with an accumulation of barnacles, clams, coral and molluscs, a scattering of gilded seashells and silver starfish, and fish scales and fishbones miraculously transformed into diamonds. The icon gives the impression of an abstract painting.

It stands close to the wide-open doors in the daylight, not in some dark glimmering corner among flickering votive candles. The clean air swirls around it. A pulpit supports it, and a sheet of glass covers it. The worshipper kisses the glass, and the priest with a cloth soaked in alcohol gently wipes the kiss away.

He was a young priest with a handsome dark face and the stocky build of a sailor, and he liked to tell stories about the icon.

"You know," he said, "the icon has been stolen several times, but it always came back to us within a day. Once in 1842 the thief succeeded in taking it as far as Andros, but the moment he stepped on land he was struck with madness. He began to shout and groan. He fell on his knees and beat his head against the earth. They say he wept tears of blood. The police were summoned and they found the icon in his luggage. He never recovered from his madness."

He spoke about these things as though they happened yesterday.

"That's why we put the icon away every night," he went on. "Every night the *Megalohari* sleeps in a column."

I wondered what to make of the odd remark until he pointed to a nearby column, and in the mysterious manner of a conjuror opened up the column to reveal a small, gleaming, chromium-plated safe inside. There were few worshippers that day; it was time for lunch and the long siesta, and he decided to put the icon away for a few hours. The column, so strangely opened, closed again, and the icon vanished.

We went out into the courtyard, among the cedars and the ornamental fountains, past the little picture gallery with its fearful collection of nineteenth century paintings, and down the marble steps toward the marble harbor. The sun came out from behind the clouds, and the town below was blinding.

The young priest caught my arm and said: "Would you like to see the torpedo?"

"What torpedo?"

"The one that sank the *Elli*. We keep it here. It has become a kind of sacred relic, to remind us of the evil in the hearts of our enemies."

In a little room near the picture gallery, facing the church, lay the black remnants of the torpedo fished out of the sea. It looked like a strange ten-foot-long black lobster with tongues and claws of iron leaping out of it, venomous still though it lay harmlessly against a wall.

Relics! So many relics that they were past counting! Lifebelts, the shattered torpedo, the skull of Pelagaya, the holy icons, the sweet-water well which was found by the workmen after they discovered the wonder-working icon, the silver and gold ex-voto offerings hanging in the church—all these suggested that very little had changed over the centuries. So it must have been in Epidaurus, Delphi and Delos long ago. Apollo had given way to Christ, Artemis and Athena had given way to the Virgin, but the trappings of worship remained constant and the hunger for relics was as insatiable as ever.

"In the church we have columns from the island of Delos," the young priest went on. "You might say they are also relics."

He showed us the columns. They were small and slender, and formed part of the colonnade facing the church. They differed from the other columns only in being more delicately carved.

In the glare of noon we walked down to the harbor ringed with its Chinese lanterns. In the white heat the blue had been drained out of the sky, the marble pavements were mirrors reflecting the light which beat interminably against the whitewashed houses, flashing from one house to another, so that in the end you almost expected the light to pulverize the whole town, turning it into dust or snow.

The young priest pointed through the incandescence to a blinding patch of sea not far from the breakwater.

"You understand, she was anchored out there. Half the crew was ashore. It was the most holy day in the year for the people of Tinos and also for the pilgrims. The ship was beflagged. Everyone was honoring the *Tiniotissa*. Then there came the sound of the explosion, and two minutes later the cruiser sank. It was no accident. It had been planned deliberately, and there was a purpose to it—it was intended to make us panic, but in fact it had the opposite effect. It steadied us. It prepared us for the war which would inevitably come. And now I ask myself, as I have asked myself so often, what madness came over the Italians that they should sink one of our ships during the feast of the Virgin?"

Samos

IN THE early morning light we steamed along the northern coast of Samos in one of those slow-moving island ships with rusted engines creaking like tin cans. We had boarded the ship at Tinos the previous night, scarcely knowing where we were going and not caring, because it is always pleasant to sail among the islands. It was a comfortable ship, heavily inlaid with Victorian furniture, with plump pillows in the cabins, an air of harmless respectability. It could have been a boarding house in London, so heavy was the furniture, so respectable the atmosphere. If the wine steward was slow and careless, it was probably because he was deafened by the uproar from the engine-room and because the ship was plunging recklessly through a small storm.

On these island ships there is never any sense of danger. You can hear the screams of the dying engine and the sound of the bottom strakes breaking apart, but danger is unthinkable. Heaven protected us. Among the ornaments of S.S. *Panteles* were two icons of the youthful St. Panteleimon, two of the aged St. Nicholas, two Annunciations, two Virgins, two medallions of Christ bearing a lamb in his arms, a vial of holy oil, and a perpetual lamp. One felt that if any of the icons were blown away, there would be enough remaining to insure the safety of our journey.

But now in the early morning light, the seas calm, the island only a ship's length away, all blue and glistening, the Victorian ship vanished and gave place to the most luxurious of modern yachts sailing in near silence along a glowing coast. From the deck Samos appeared like a virgin land, and the ship itself, washed down by the crew, appeared to be on its maiden voyage. The rattle of the engine-room had long ago died down, as though in homage to the beauty of the morning. Samos is not like Delos, which lies only a few inches above the surface of the sea. It is huge and mountainous, with powerful hunched shoulders, muscular and taut, with forests growing on its precipitous slopes. There are farmhouses high up, reached by the faint white pathways scored on the sheer rocks. Samos is a Phoenician word, meaning "high" or "huge"; and it was well-named. More than any other Greek island it gives from the sea an impression of resolute power.

When Athens was young, Samos was already a power to be reckoned with. The grandeur of the island seems to have been communicated to its first settlers, who came perhaps from Argos. They were a proud and defiant people, freebooters and philosophers, poets and artists, architects and engineers without peer in the ancient world. Pythagoras was a Samian; so too was Aristarchus, the first to suggest that the earth revolved round the sun, and not the sun round the earth. The philosopher Epicurus was a Samian, and so was Conon, the teacher of Archimedes. The Samian sailor Coleos was the first Greek to reach the Atlantic Ocean. It was a Samian, Mandocles, who bridged the Bosphorus to enable the army of Darius to cross into Europe and fight against the Scythians. The muster roll of great Samians was an impressive one, though it includes many like the historians Douris and Dionysios who are known only by reputation. If Crete saw the beginning of European civilization, then Samos saw the beginning of the scientific spirit. Crete, Samos, and Athens in that order are the founding fathers of the West, and we are their children.

So one gazes at that robust and steep-sided island almost with a sense of familiarity, admiring the power and effrontery of the mountains in the pure breath of the morning air. The sky was a darker blue than we were accustomed to see in the western islands. With a shock we realized that the coasts of Asia were only a few miles away. Already we were in the Orient.

At last the island steamer curls into a sheltered harbor in the northeastern corner of the island. Red-tiled houses form a semi-circle around the bay, reaching up toward the top of the red earth hills. It is a modern town, strangely un-Greek in appearance, and there are no ancient forts, no temples in sight. In fact the town, which is called Vathy, was built by the Turks barely a hundred years ago. It has a new, freshly painted look, the streets clean, the people plump, the air sweet. Men and women were going about their affairs briskly, for the island has never become a tourist center and there was no self-conscious gaping at strangers. Vathy was trying to become a modern town, and with its harbor, its factories and distilleries it was largely succeeding.

When I think of Vathy I remember the fresh morning air scented with pines and thyme blowing through the narrow, winding streets which, in spite of their Turkish appearance, reminded me of the Latin quarter in Paris. Greek architecture had vanished; there were no whitewashed, flat-roofed Cycladic houses, no outside stairways, nothing to suggest that this was an island in the Aegean. There were excellent cafés, where they served the finest Turkish coffee I tasted in Greece, and the restaurants for once were impeccably clean. There was a delightful square shaded by palm trees and named after Pythagoras, but there was no statue of the great mathematician and scientist; instead there was a replica of the Lion of Chaeronea reduced in scale so that it had lost its ferocity and resembled a cat.

The truth is that Vathy is essentially bourgeois, a town of merchants and lawyers interested in their creature comforts, dependent on trade for its living. It had a *crowded* look, while even Rhodes and Heracleion wear a distressing air of emptiness, as though they were waiting for something to happen and had not yet come to terms with the ghosts of the past. Vathy has no past worth speaking of, and can therefore look briskly to the future.

We had been on the island three minutes when Mr. Stergos Horatiopoulos took charge of us. He was an unlikely guide, plump, affable and knowledgeable, an Alexandrian Greek who had married a woman of Samos and had no interest in delivering lectures on antiquity. His function as he saw it was to guide, to see that the museums were opened for us and that we would eat reasonably well and that we would find reasonably inexpensive taxis. He only once mentioned the name of Polycrates. This was a feat of considerable magnitude, since the guidebooks speak of scarcely anyone else, and all the great works of art and all the great engineering constructions of Samos are associated with his name. When we asked to see a distillery, he took us to the largest distillery on the island, and then discreetly hovered in the background, only insisting that we should drink as many wines as possible. The two museums were closed. He opened both of them with a wave of his magic hand. On the rare occasions when he mentioned a date, it was accurate. To anyone who has listened to Greek guides such quietness, reserve and accuracy appear almost miraculous.

Still, there was no escape from Polycrates. He was inscribed across the awnings, he was in the street signs, a wine had been named after him, and soon there will be a hotel. Herodotus, who has provided the best of all guidebooks to the islands, and who lived in Samos in his youth and might have told us more had his interest in politics been stronger, tells the story of how Polycrates son of Aeaces seized the citadel with fifteen hoplites, and after sharing his power for a while with his two brothers, killed one of them and exiled the other. With the help of the tyrant Lygdamis of Naxos he established himself firmly in power, conquered many islands, allied himself with Egypt, and fought the Persians. He must have had a special affection for Apollo, for he conquered Rheneia and solemnly dedicated this island to the god. He invited the greatest poets of his time to his court, and lived sumptuously and splendidly. But what he was chiefly famous for was his impudent good luck.

Herodotus tells a beguiling story about the famous luck of Polycrates as it was viewed by Amasis, the king of Egypt:

Amasis was fully aware of the extraordinary good fortune of Polycrates, and it caused him a certain amount of uneasiness. When he heard of these ever-mounting successes, he wrote the following letter and sent it to Samos: "Amasis to Polycrates—it is always a pleasure to hear of a friend and an ally acquiring prosperity, but I can scarcely rejoice at your continuing good fortune, knowing as I do that the gods are always envious of success. My own wish, both for those I care for and for myself, would be to do well in some things and badly in others, thus passing through life amid alternations of success and failure, rather than to live a life of unmitigated triumph. For I have never yet heard of a man who after an unbroken run of luck has not finally been brought to absolute ruin. Now I would like to suggest that you meet your good fortune in the following way. Think of the most valuable of your treasures, whatever you would most hate to lose, and throw it away in such a fashion that it will never again be seen by mortal eyes. Then, if your good fortune does not take a turn for the worse, take more doses of the medicine I have advised."

Polycrates read the letter and observed that there was considerable truth in the warning of Amasis, and looked around among his treasures for the one he most hated to lose. Finally he decided that it was a signet ring, set in gold with an emerald, the work of Theodoros, the son of Telecles, a Samian. Having decided that this was the treasure he would have to dispose of, he manned a fifty-oared ship, went aboard, and gave orders to the sailors to put to sea. When the ship was a long way from Samos, he took the ring from his finger in full view of everyone on board, and threw it into the water. Then he was rowed back to his house, and lamented the lost treasure.

We can almost guess the rest of the story. A few days later a fisherman caught a magnificent fish and decided that it was altogether too good to be sold on the open market; he took it to the tyrant and offered it as a gift. Polycrates was pleased, accepted the fish, ordered the servants to prepare it, and was not unduly surprised when they discovered the ring inside the fish. "You see, my luck holds," he wrote to Amasis, and Amasis, more than ever afraid of the inevitable retribution which would be exacted by the gods, promptly broke the treaty of alliance between them. The judgment of Amasis was vindicated a few years later when Oroetes, the satrap of Sardis, lured Polycrates to the mainland, ambushed him and skinned him alive. What was left after he had been skinned was hung on a cross.

So died Polycrates, but the memory of his magnificence endured. His fleet of a hundred penteconters roamed the eastern Mediterranean, his palaces and temples decorated the capital, and the greatest poets of his time celebrated his glory. He had a genuine delight in the arts, and he was one of those rare beings, like Lorenzo de' Medici, who possessed exquisite taste and built for all time. Even today, among the gladioli and the thistles of a marshy shore, there can be seen the altars he erected to the goddess Hera, who protected him while he remained on the island, only to abandon him when he set foot in a foreign land.

A Gift for Apollo

"The museum is closed," Mr. Horatiopoulos announced, when we drove to the small dusty sidestreet in Tigani, the village which occupies a corner of the site of Polycrates' ancient capital.

"Then what do we do?"

"We open it," he said, and then vanished, only to reappear mysteriously a few moments later with the key.

It was a sad little museum, consisting of two rooms and a corridor, smelling of plaster and decay, unventilated, rarely entered. On the walls were fly-specked engravings of the Greek captains who fought against the Turks in the nineteenth century, some ancient funerary steles, busts of ancient Romans remarkable only because so many were without noses and seemed therefore without character or expression. Even if they had possessed noses, they would not have filled us with enthusiasm.

Nowhere except in some local museums in England and France, where the spiders weave heavy webs over the cases of Roman coins and the stuffed alligators, have I seen such a tawdry display. Whatever life there had been in the museum had been snuffed out long ago except for one brilliant living object, which had survived through twenty-five centuries. This was a life-size statue of Hera enthroned, attended by her guardian lions, which stood in the front room close to the window. She was headless, but still powerful. Time had smoothed out the heavy folds of her garments, worn away her fingers and her feet, but she remained powerful and vigorous still. She was full-breasted, as befits the wife of Zeus, and imperious, as befits the guardian goddess of an island as powerful as

Samos. The statue was of biscuit-colored stone, and had evidently stood in one of the earlier temples of Hera. An inscription in archaic lettering announces that the statue was presented by Aeaces to Hera and paid for out of the spoils of war or from the plunder of a pirate raid—the troubling word *syle* can be read clearly, but its exact meaning is still unknown. It can mean spoils, plunder, booty, even perhaps wealth acquired by force or by threats of force, which was the most desirable wealth in the eyes of the Samian tyrants. The word appears also as an element in the name of Syloson, the brother of Polycrates. The inscription is worn, but most of the letters are still clearly visible. Even if there was no inscription, it would be evident that this was the statue of a great and powerful goddess carved at a time of assurance and conquest. She was characteristically Samian, with that rather heavy, smoothed-out, monumental appearance which is always found in the age of Polycrates.

So there she was, sitting enthroned in the front room of a house no larger than a workman's dwelling, with the plaster falling from the ceiling, and no one traveling along that street would have guessed that this was a museum containing a great and venerable object which would be regarded as a treasure in any of the world's museums. The monumental art of Samos has almost entirely perished, and we can only guess at the achievements of the reign of Polycrates from a few surviving masterpieces. The sculptures of Samos have shared the fate of those of Aegina, for most of the rare survivors have been scattered abroad.

In Vathy there is another museum, which did not in the least resemble a workman's dwelling place. It was a small palace designed with taste in a secluded garden shaded by palm trees. It might have been the summer house of some immensely wealthy landed proprietor near Paris. Instead it was the repository of some of the most exciting sculptures to be seen on the Greek islands.

We came to the museum at midday, and as we had half-expected, it was closed. Mr. Horatiopoulos waved his magic wand and a young curator appeared from nowhere. He wore a heavy dark suit, though it was one of those sweltering hot windless summer days which send the inhabitants of Vathy running to the hills. He had a lean narrow face with thick dark eyebrows, and was very nearly as handsome as some of the sculptures in the museum. He was polite, informative and intelligent, wore his learning lightly, and had no objection to photographers. After a while he said: "The museum is yours," and then vanished discreetly into the background.

It is impossible not to write about the museum at Vathy with affection. Everything about it was designed to please the eye. It is not particularly spacious, but it gives an impression of spaciousness. It is well arranged, the walls are painted in pastel shades, and full use has been made of the staircase, with sculptures inset in niches in the most advantageous position for anyone climbing the stairs. It has great treasures, among them three figures from the design known as the Arcade of Geneleos. This was a group of detached figures found in the sanctuary of Hera about 1875, of which the most famous was carried off to the Louvre and two others went to Berlin. The museum at Vathy has the three remaining figures: a seated Hera, a young goddess, and a reclining figure of unknown sex, for most of it has been destroyed. The Hera and the goddess are both headless. The sculptor has carved the word "Philippe" on the goddess, who is depicted with her hands pulling at her skirt so that the very fine plaits are widened and curved as they fall to her feet. "Philippe" is probably the name of the model, for there is no doubt that the statue represents a goddess. These three statues, with the stone platform on which they have always rested, occupy the full length of the room on the ground floor of the museum.

Upstairs, looking out on the gardens, there is the broken remnant of a funerary stele, very bright in the sunlight. A naked youth has come to say farewell to his dead mother or sister; we see only her knees. He carries her jewel-case and is evidently about to present her with one of the jewels. It is a theme which is often repeated in Greek funerary steles. The mourning figures are usually clothed, for the beauty of flesh has little enough to do with the contemplation of death. Here the sculptor has simply abandoned the acceptable tradition, and made the leave-taking all the more poignant by depicting a curly-headed youth of great beauty bidding farewell to the woman seated in front of him. His soft chin, fine curls and languid grace suggest that he is perfectly aware of his beauty while at the same time helplessly aware of grief. It is a late work, probably Hellenistic, and leaves one with a slight uneasiness, so brutal is the contrast between his glowing flesh and the dead woman to whom he offers a last tribute of affection.

Downstairs in the hallway is a marble kouros of even greater beauty, for it is more robust and the breath of life flows through it. It can be dated about 530 B.C., when the stylized archaic forms were giving way to forms filled with the sense of movement and power. This kouros knows where he is going, for Apollo has blessed him. Indeed, he must have graced a temple to Apollo, for there is an inscription on his left thigh which reads: "EUKIOS DEDICATED ME TO APOLLO." So he stands there, confident in his youth, beautiful in the thrust of his young body, the most Apollonian of all the sculptures we saw in the islands.

The Tunnel of Eupalinos

"I have dwelt," says Herodotus, "longer on the affairs of the Samians than I should otherwise have done, because they are responsible for three of the greatest building and engineering feats in all Greece. The first is a tunnel nearly a mile long, eight feet wide and eight feet high, driven clear through the base of a hill nine hundred feet high. Along the whole course there is a second cutting thirty feet deep and three feet broad, and along this cutting water from an abundant source is led through pipes into the city. The architect of the tunnel was Eupalinos, son of Naustrophos of Megara. The second is an artificial harbor enclosed by a breakwater, which runs out into twenty fathoms of water and has a total length of one thousand, two hundred feet. The third is a temple, the largest known to us. The first architect was Rhoecos, son of Phileos, a Samian. These three works seem to me of sufficient merit to justify a rather longer discussion of the affairs of Samos."

So spoke Herodotus, who knew Samos well, for it was on this island in his younger years that he learned to speak the Ionic dialect. He was a man who liked to tell legendary stories, the more miraculous the better, but in his brief account of the three greatest building and engineering feats in Greece he was telling no more than the truth. To this day we can see the tunnel of Eupalinos, and though the breakwater is submerged below the sea, we can still see its outlines and trace its contours. As for the temple of Hera, it was 354 feet long, 175 feet wide, and was supported by 134 columns. Such a vast display of columns suggests an Egyptian influence, and in fact Samos was in close contact with Egypt from remote periods of antiquity.

The temple seen by Herodotus was the fourth and last to be erected on this spot, the others having been destroyed by fire. Curiously, Herodotus says nothing about the architect Theodoros reputed to have been the designer of the temple, with Rhoecos acting merely as his assistant. Theodoros was the architect of the vast temple of Artemis in Ephesus, which was ordered by King Croesos of Lydia. The Artemision was the most sumptuous temple of that age, perhaps of all ages, and the Heraion was quite simply the largest temple ever built by the Greeks. That forest of columns earned it the name of "the Labyrinth."

Today nothing remains of the Heraion except one solitary white column and acres of ruins hidden in the long marsh grass, such a welter of drums and blocks of marble that you find yourself wondering whether the temple might not have been a mile long. For twenty-five centuries the temple has been plundered. Drums from the columns litter the harbor; decorative capitals stand outside houses and are used as flower vases; broken pieces of the columns have become bollards. The town of Tigani glows with its ancient marbles.

The archaeologists have mapped the ruins. They know where the Great Altar stands; they have marked out the sacred road and the tribune which is called after Cicero, because he may have spoken from this spot, and they think they know where the Mycenaean wall ran; and now after fifty years the excavations are over, and the long field stretching to the sea looks strangely empty, as though the ghosts have all gone home.

Year after year, one season after another, the Germans came

The church of the Paraportiani at Myconos.
Two Hellenistic statues at Delos.
Archaic lioness at Delos.
The cave of Dikte from inside.
The throne of Homer at Chios.
Unfinished archaic kouros at Naxos.
Hellenistic grave stele in the museum at Vathy.
Kouros in the museum at Vathy.

here and dug prodigiously and found little, for the site had been raided for centuries before they came. The immense temple under the half-bowl of mountains eluded them, though they succeeded in mapping a vast area of ruins. The temple even eluded its builders, for it was never completed. The Athenians invaded the island; then came Alexander, in whose time the last unfluted columns were put up. It is marshy ground, thick with poppies, gladioli and feathery thistles, and sometimes as you walk there you can feel under your heels the shock of marble still buried in the earth. In fifty years the Germans could not have dug up more than a corner of that vast marshy plain.

For centuries the city of Polycrates survived, becoming at last a Roman city. Here came Antony and Cleopatra to rejoice in their good fortune at finding one another and to celebrate the coming war with Augustus Caesar, then still known as Octavian, for he had not yet conquered the lovers and by conquering them conquered the world. Antony and Cleopatra were so sure of their strength and of the eventual downfall of Octavian that they took a long holiday in Samos and gave themselves up to a perpetual round of feasts and entertainments. Plutarch tells the story:

> *When all their forces were joined together, they hoisted sail for the island of Samos, and gave themselves up to feasting and entertainments. Previously they had ordered that all the kings, princes and governors, and all the nations and cities within the frontiers of Syria, the Maeotid Lake, Armenia and Illyria should bring together or cause to be brought together all munitions necessary for the conduct of war, and now they issued another order—they proclaimed that all the players,*

minstrels, tumblers, fools and jesters should appear before them at Samos. So it happened that while every other place in the world was filled with groans and lamentations, on this island alone there was to be heard for many days the music of pipes and harps, and theaters full of actors, and choruses singing. Every city sent an ox as a gift to the festivity, and the kings who were in Antony's retinue competed with one another as to who would offer the most magnificent feasts or present the most valuable gifts, so that men began to ask themselves how, after such an expense of feasting before the war began, they would be able to celebrate the victory when it was over.

As we know, there was no victory, and Antony and Cleopatra went down to defeat, having lost an empire for dallying so long on Samos.

In Roman times Samos continued to be a great city, famous for its wine, its pottery and its climate. We know that the palace of Polycrates fell into ruins, for Caligula planned to restore it. Hadrian, too, lingered in this imperial city and rejoiced in its pleasant airs. Under the Byzantine empire it retained its importance as a naval base, for it was from this harbor that Nicephoros Phocas sailed against Crete, to make it one more jewel in the Byzantine crown. When Constantinople at last fell to the Turks, Samos was abandoned by the Greeks, who fled to Chios, Lesbos and the mainland of Greece. Then for two centuries Samos became a desert, the haunt of corsairs and pirates. Gradually the Greeks returned and established themselves on the island, making life unendurable for the Turks, their nominal masters, who spoke of "going to Samos" when they meant "going to their deaths." By 1832 the Samians were able to exact home rule from the Turks. They were ruled by a Christian prince and an elected house of representatives until 1912, when they finally broke free of Turkey and united with Greece. No other island under Turkish rule ever wrested so much freedom from the enemy.

Today it is still the island of Polycrates, of whose works only one remains intact—the tunnel driven by Eupalinos through the mountain, which was rediscovered in 1878. It was a little narrower than Herodotus had described it, and together with the main tunnel there was a kind of slot on one side of it, two feet deep and nine inches wide, through which the waters ran. The main tunnel was about five feet six inches high and five feet wide, very damp and slippery, but not particularly dangerous. Here and there it opens out into small galleries. Clearly it was not merely an aqueduct, for it had other uses. It provided a means of escape from the city, for Herodotus tells us that after Polycrates was crucified, the Persians assisted Syloson to recover the island and Maeandrios the local tyrant fled "through a secret underground passage leading from the citadel to the sea." But the tunnel could very well serve many other purposes. Treasure could be hidden in it, and some of the galleries which can be found at intervals along the length of the cave could serve as prisons. Burial ground, prison, treasure-chest, escape route—it was all these. The brilliant engineering feat could be put to terrible uses.

A motor road now reaches up the side of Mount Castro to the mouth of the tunnel. You step down five steps, open a little green gate, and you are in the tunnel which goes in a straight line for more than three thousand feet. The air is sweet, and only a little water seeps through the rock. It is a strangely comfortable place as long as the flashlight is turned on, the tunnel gleaming silver, but oppressive and horrible the moment it is turned off. An immense silence then wells out of the living rock; and from far away, giving weight to the silence, comes the sound of slowly trickling water.

Over the years there have been rockfalls, subsidences and earthquakes, but the shape of the tunnel has remained unaltered; only the ceramic water pipes have been shattered. You kneel down and plunge your arm into the little trench beside the roadway, and it is full of broken pipes. There was once more than a mile of pipes, for the spring feeding the aqueduct was some distance from the northern entrance to the tunnel. Now nothing remains except these red shards littering the little trench.

By the light of a torch the tunnel is oddly friendly, and this comes, I think, from its sculptural appearance, the unevenness of the walls, the interminable brisk marks of pickaxes and chisels on the walls, the sense of human effort. It has been calculated that a thousand slaves working with the available instruments would have taken fifteen years to complete the tunnel. No doubt they were treated abominably, and every foot of the tunnel was attended by tragedy. Yet, as you wander into the tunnel's depths, you become aware of the human grandeur written on the walls as well as the savagery of the enterprise. And when at last you emerge from the tunnel, all Samos seems to be on fire.

The Blue Fountains of Air

There are times when one can grow weary of the islands, when the jeweled brilliance of the colors makes one ache for a more diffuse and colorless landscape, when Paradise becomes a prison. Suddenly and unexpectedly you find yourself dreaming of London or New York on a dark winter's day, when the richest color is the silvery grey of a rain-soaked street. After so many days in the sun you yearn for the comfort of mists and the smoke of autumn. Too much splendor ends in satiety: too many golden swords are flashing in the sky. You understand at last why Adam and Eve escaped from the garden.

Still, there are degrees of splendor. *Splendidus, splendidior, splendidissimus,* and this is only the beginning, for there are a multitude of inching steps along that ladder. I thought the most splendid place of all was Lindos until I came to Samos and discovered that Christian monks knew at least as much about splendor as the ancient Greeks. On a road in Samos, overlooking the mountains of Turkey, with no man-made buildings or columns in sight, you meet the goddess face to face, wearing her most glorious raiments.

The monks who founded the monastery of Our Lady, the Fountain of Life, in 1756 knew what they were doing. They built a rather commonplace monastery resembling a square fortress on the cliffs overlooking the sea. It was light and airy within the walls, all blue and white, with wooden galleries running round the courts. It was not a rich monastery. Unlike the Monastery of the Holy Girdle some distance away, it possessed no valuable relics, and indeed its only possession of any worth was an icon of St. Anne holding the Virgin in her arms. The icon, like so many others in Greek churches, lies in a hammered silver shroud, with only the holy faces still visible, but an artist has engraved on the silver a representation of the rich and swirling vestments which lie beneath. Those tumultuous and balanced swirls suggest the waves of the sea.

But it is not for the monastery or even for the wonder-working icon that one walks along the steep path zigzagging up the side of the mountain. It is a wide road with a stone wall, and no doubt there are cars which enjoy climbing at an angle of forty-five degrees, but our car simply refused to make the journey. We were going to the monastery for no particular reason except that we liked its name, the Fountain of Life, and we had no idea what was in store. Suddenly at a turning in the road, beyond the pines and the carob trees and the sloping red and yellow earth, we saw the sea, but this was no ordinary sea. It was the royal blue of Lindos, but unimaginably richer because it was contained within a circle formed by the mountains of Samos and Turkey. This was blue with depths upon depths of gold, so dark, so rich, so filled with fire that it seemed to belong to some other earth than any we had known. This was the ultimate blue, and it was worth traveling to Samos for no other reason than to see that blue sea set among the blue mountains.

The effect was of an incomparable grandeur deliberately designed, as though those mountains and the wandering coast had been built by an enchanting artist. There was an impression of stillness, but also of stately movement as waves of misty golden blue rode up the sides of the mountains. From the heart of the blue lake fountains of air seemed to be rising and falling away; the landscape was bathed in blue fire.

We walked up the pathway like crabs, sideways, unable to tear our eyes away from those swirling pools and fountains of a blue more royal than any we ever hoped to see. The sea was calm with no wavecaps, but on these heights the wind blew keenly, and the soughing of the pines accompanied the swirling of the blue air. There was the scent of hay, of thyme and pine needles. Everything about the scene, even the reddish-yellow earth and the fan-shaped carob trees, seemed to be acting in unison to display the blue to its greatest advantage.

This was Galilee transported to the edge of Asia, and yet more beautiful than Galilee. In the time of Christ, when the shores of Galilee were thick with trees, the lake must have been a deeper blue than it is today beneath the eroded mountains. Galilee is silvery blue, and there are no blue fountains of air rising from its depths. Here, facing Cape Mycale, the blue is so laced with gold that it acquires something more than splendor; it acquires majesty.

From where the monks look out of their windows, the scene is one of intense drama, although in human terms nothing is happening. There are no armies contending for power, and only rarely do ships sail past the cape. What is dramatic is the appearance of majesty rising perpetually from a blue sea.

Here, on just such a summer day, on August 27, 479 B.C., there occurred an event which went far to shape the destiny of Europe. The Persian fleet was lying at anchor off Samos when a small Greek fleet found them. Fearing a revolt by the Samians, the Persians withdrew to Cape Mycale on the mainland where they beached their ships and built a stockade of stones and tree trunks to defend them. Toward evening the Greek fleet, composed mostly of Athenian and Spartan ships, sailed offshore. The commander of the fleet was Leotychides, king of Sparta, and he ordered a herald to shout across the waters to the Ionian Greeks still serving with the Persians: "Men of Ionia, when the battle begins, let each of you first remember Freedom, and then remember Hera, who is our watchword!" At night the Greeks attacked the Persian stockade and set fire to the beached ships. The Persians fled; the Ionian Greeks rose in revolt; the ships of Leotychides sailed north to the Hellespont to cut off the retreat of the Persians defeated on the Greek mainland, for on that same day the Greeks had won a victory over the Persian army in Boeotia. Now with the destruction of the Persians at Mycale their victory was complete. "Remember Freedom and Hera!" The burned ships at Mycale were a watchword and a sign; and the threat of Persia vanished like the morning dew.

Now all is peaceful in the straits of Samos, and only rare visitors walk up the zigzag pathway to the monastery of Our Lady, the Fountain of Life, where there can be seen the loveliest view in all Greece.

Chios

ONE MORNING, when the sea was like a glassy lake, we glided into Chios on a little rusted tramp steamer laden with more drums of olive oil than I ever thought a tramp steamer could carry. Evidently the drums were leaking, for my memories of Chios are filled with the reek of olive oil. Manoli, the ship's captain, said he would be sailing to Lesbos later in the day, but he was uncertain about the time—it might be in the evening or at night or the next day. It appeared that he had some business to attend to in the town, or maybe there was no business. He shrugged his shoulders. "It will be as God wills," he said, and he looked through the porthole with the expression of a man who finds little comfort in the uncertainties of island trade.

He was a small man with bushy eyebrows and a face of red leather, squat and broad-shouldered, and I thought he moved ponderously until I saw him leaping from the bow across six feet of water to the jetty. He was an emperor in his cabin, stern and decisive, barking out orders to the ship's boys as though they were slaves, but he was kinder to the man at the ship's wheel who was growing blind and making his last voyage. In his cabin, slipped into wooden racks overhead, were the worn maps he rarely consulted, for he knew the Aegean as well as he knew the back of his hand. The cabin was bare like the man, stripped to essentials. We knew the cabin well, for we had spent the night in it, each of us lying on a narrow bench while the captain snored in his bunk; and all through the night I thought I heard the rivets sheering off and falling into the sea. Now in the early morning, the sea calm, Chios within sight, we asked him about the island—where to go, and what were the best wines, and how the people lived. Suddenly he looked worn and old, and threw up his hands in a gesture of despair.

"How should I know?" he said. "I don't live there."

"But you've been here before. Surely you know the island?"

"I know nothing about it. I don't go wandering round the island. I'm a ship's captain, and I look after my ship, and see the ship chandlers, and do business in the port, and that's all I do. I have a wife and family in Salonica, and if you ask me about Salonica, I could tell you something about the town, and about where to eat and what to see, but God knows what there is in Chios. They say Homer was born there."

"And was he?"

"God knows, I wasn't present at his birth."

He smiled then, but the smile faded quickly as he went on to explain that ships' captains knew little enough about the islands. He never went into a town, never saw anyone unconnected with trade, never stayed longer than a few hours, a day at the most. His aim was to drop into a port and pull out in the shortest possible time. In that way, always making up for lost time, he was able to serve the shipowners and save himself a few extra hours in Salonica whenever he returned home. He reckoned he spent twenty days a year in Salonica. For the rest of the year he was sailing among the islands. He made two thousand dollars a year. The ship's boys made thirty dollars a month. It was a hard life, but in his gruff sea captain's way he seemed to revel in it.

We left the tramp steamer, not knowing whether we would ever see it again, for he was exasperatingly vague about the time of departure. He told us he would leave our bags on the jetty if we returned too late.

In the dawnlight Chios was grey and shadowy under its minarets, and uninviting. Dawn seemed to climb wearily through streets as empty as the streets of French provincial towns. It was a small town clustered on the waterfront, and no doubt it would be bright enough at noon, but now it seemed to be drugged by nightmares. There was no one about. Then we saw a lamb with a string round its neck being led to the slaughterhouse, and we knew the day had begun.

Sometimes, turning into a narrow alleyway, we thought we were back in the Turkish quarter of Rhodes, for the Turkish influence was strong in the fretted doorways and the way the streets wound in serpentine fashion. Yet Rhodes preserved its dignity, while Chios was shabby and down at heel, having almost forgotten its past. Once it was wealthy. There was a time when fortunes were made in gum mastic, turpentine and wine. Gum mastic, the resin from the terebinth tree, was the island's most valuable product, exported all over the world, possessing so many providential uses that it re-

sembled the bamboo in China: it could be made into almost anything one pleased. It was a base for paints and varnish and chewing
gum and cosmetics and dental creams; it was a medicine; it was
used in the textile industry and by lithographers and by bakers; and
its essential oils were used in liqueurs. The Chians grew fat on gum
mastic and built themselves great estates, until the synthetic gums
and varnishes came in. Then they were ruined. Now the islanders
complain that Athens has forgotten them, and no tourists come,
and there is almost no trade.

Three hundred years ago the women of Chios were famous for
their beauty and a certain lightmindedness. William Lithgow, who
traveled to Chios in 1610, was pleasantly surprised to find them so
accommodating, and described them in his travel book, *The Total
Discourse of the Rare Adventures and Painefull Peregrinations of
Long Nineteene Years Travayles from Scotland to the most King-
doms in Europe, Asia and Affrica*. He wrote:

> *The Women of the Citty are the most beautifull Dames, (or
> rather Angelicall creatures) of all the Greekes, upon the face
> of the earth, and greatly given to Venery. They are for the
> most part exceeding proude, and sumptuous in aparell, and
> commonly go (even Artificers wives) in gowns of Sattin and
> Taffety; yea, in Cloth of Silver and Gold, and are adorned with
> precious Stones, and Gemmes, and Jewels about their neckes,
> and hands, with Rings, Chaines, & Bracelets. Their Husbands
> are their Pandors, and when they see any stranger arrive, they
> will presently demaund of him; if he would have a Mistresse:
> and so they made Whoores of their own Wives, and are con-
> tented for a little gaine, to wear hornes: such are the base minds*

of ignominious Cuckolds. If a Straunger be desirous to stay all night with any of them, their price is a Chicken of Gold, nine Shillings English, out of which this companion receiveth his supper, and for his paines, a belly full of sinful content.

But though we searched in Chios for these angelical women adorned with precious stones and gems and jewels about their necks, we found none; only hard-working peasant girls burned dark by the sun.

We wandered through the drab streets where the only color came from the disemboweled sheep, black with flies, hanging in the butchers' shops; there was the smell of fresh blood and open sewers. The museum, too, was drab, dusty, without color or excitement. A mosque had been deconsecrated and converted into a repository for all the unimportant odds and ends discovered on the island. There were plaster casts of famous statues found in Chios, long since removed to Athens and Paris. Hanging from the dome was an execrable fly-spotted copy of Delacroix's *Massacre at Chios*. The wind blew through the holes of the canvas, which hung limply like the sail of a ship abandoned on a forgotten coast.

The Fiery Colors

There is a church on the island of Chios blazing with color, high in the mountains, lost among olive groves, far from any human habitation. The eagles wheel above it, and the sea lies so far below that the church, though inland, gives the impression of being perched on a cliff like the great temple at Lindos. It is very quiet in these uplands, the silence broken occasionally by the deep-voiced chanting of an old priest, the murmuring of waters and the ringing of sheep bells. The air is pure there, and the springs have a sweet taste.

They call the place Nea Moni, the new monastery, a name it has borne for more than nine hundred years. The story goes that the mountain caught fire, and three hermits wandering among the burned-out stumps of trees found a myrtle tree untouched by the flames, with a wonder-working icon of the Virgin hanging from one of the branches. At that time Constantine Monomachus was in exile on the island of Lesbos. The hermits sought out the young prince and obtained his promise to build a church on the mountains whenever he became emperor. Some forty years later, in 1042 A.D., he came to the throne. The hermits then reminded him of his promise. He ordered his architects to build a church on the spot where the icon was found, and he sent his artists to paint the walls in glittering mosaics. It was to be a jewel-box to hold the wonder-working icon. So it came about that the island of Chios contains to this day mosaics fashioned by artists of the Byzantine court.

On none of the other islands of the Aegean are there any Byzantine mosaics. You come upon frescoes in all the islands, and some of the best of them are to be found on an ancient hill in Aegina, but not mosaics by the supreme masters of the art. These imperial mosaics had rich colors, elegance, a royal refinement, a wonderful assurance. The fiery colors glowed, the crowded figures possessed a life of their own and seemed to breathe, and Christ in glory and in rainbow colors peered down from the dome with a fierce magnificence. There was a time when they made jewel-boxes of all their churches. Outside: red roofs and stucco walls. Inside: the fuming, blinding light of thousands upon thousands of pieces of colored glass.

The Byzantines practiced the art with a superb sense of the fitness of small pieces of colored glass to represent the divine and the eternal. They calculated to a hairbreadth the reflective power of those glass beads, which became their brush strokes. Whole walls became cascades of jewels reflecting the heavenly light.

Until recently only a winding mule track led into the mountains and it was a full day's journey to the lonely church of Nea Moni. Now there is a road of sorts, scratched out of the mountain's ribs, with hundred-foot drops at every turning.

Our driver, Kimon, had a dark olive skin and beetle brows and a thin mustache, which gave him something of the appearance of a hero in a Victorian novel. He wore a leather jacket, but he would look well enough in the uniform of an officer of the guards. He was born without a sense of danger and with a gift of uninterrupted and uninterruptable speech, and he liked to gesticulate with both hands. He told stories well, but he was the worst driver I have ever known.

He especially liked to test the edge of the road, daring it to give way. He had other foibles. He liked to turn his head and contemplate the scenery behind, pointing to its various excellencies and its innumerable horrors, while driving at sixty miles an hour. It amused him to denounce Karamanlis and all the other prime ministers who have ruled over Greece since the age of Themistocles, but his special hatred was reserved for the local shipowners and their wives who built their palaces on the seashore, surrounded themselves with luxury, and took no interest in the fate of the islanders.

Kimon had many stories about them. The best was about the rich widow of a shipowner who built an enormous church as a passport to Paradise, and when asked to contribute money to the making of needed roads, answered: "You dare to ask me for money for roads when I have built you a church?"

"You ought to see that church," Kimon said. "No one ever goes there—she saw to that. There are four priests, and they each pray for her soul for six hours a day. The villagers starve, but there is enough money for prayers to be said for her to eternity."

He went on to tell other stories about the shipowners, while skirting the edge of the white road and always speeding at hairpin bends. At last the road straightened out, the olive groves began, and the small red-domed church appeared in the nest of the mountain. It was a very small church, in shape like hundreds of other Byzantine churches, but the site was enchanting with the wild scarp of Mount Provation behind, while below there was only greenness cascading down to the sea. White goats were tumbling in the olive groves. The air smelled of thyme and sweetness, and the bells were ringing.

They told us in Chios that Nea Moni was falling to ruins and there was only a solitary priest living there, but it was not in ruins and the old priest with the apple cheeks and the long white forked beard was not solitary, for some seven or eight nuns were singing the responses. They looked like farm women in disguise, but they sang lustily in their drab, black robes. The sun poured through the windows, and there was the smell of hay inside the church. I have seen churches in Athens which have a more abandoned look.

Nea Moni is not Daphni, where the art of the mosaicist reached its greatest heights, yet the mosaics, cracked by earthquakes and discolored by time, possess an astonishing delicacy and refinement. They seem to hang on the walls by frail threads—a puff of wind will bring them down. Yet the fiery colors glow, splashed here and there over the walls of the katholikon and the narthex, wherever they have been permitted to remain. They have survived by a miracle, for Chios is particularly prone to earthquakes. Indeed, all the mosaics survived until 1881 when a particularly devastating earthquake struck the island. In that year the dome fell, and the mosaic of Christ within the dome was completely ruined. What survives is the remnant of a remnant, but there is enough to tell us that an artist of great sensibility and uncommon imagination worked on the mosaics. It is the same in Daphni, the emptiness of the walls and the sudden splashes of fiery color.

We do not know the name of the artist, and in fact we very rarely know the names of the mosaicists. We know the names of the three hermits who found the wonder-working icon. They were John, Joseph and Niketas, and their portraits, apparently taken from life, remain. Niketas is especially impressive with his severe, watchful, youthful features, wearing a sea-blue robe, one hand uplifted in blessing, but one remembers most his watchfulness: he is guarding his treasure. Of the ten or eleven fragments that remain, the most beautiful is the Resurrection or Descent into Limbo, where Christ stands in the center in an attitude of grave authority, holding a Cross in one hand and with the other summoning Adam to emerge from his grave in a golden mountain. Adam, weighed down with years, kneels heavily and seems to be groping blindly. Eve, however, is erect, in full command of herself, and very young. Following the pattern established for the representation of the Resurrection King David and King Solomon, wearing jeweled crowns and golden haloes, gaze tranquilly at the dead rising from the earth. They seem to be holding a watching brief for royalty.

The colors still shine freshly, and they seem to hover over the surface a quarter of an inch away from the walls. Christ's gown is patterned in gold. He stands against a gold sunrise. The garments of the dead are sprinkled with jewels, and King David and King Solomon wear the jeweled garments of Byzantine emperors. Coral, pink, sea-blue, gold, black and white are painted into the gowns, which acquire purely abstract patterns.

Nearby is the Crucifixion, Christ beheaded by an earthquake, wearing a robe of dazzling splendor. The three Marys stand on the left in attitudes of overwhelming sorrow, somber and austere witnesses of a death so heavy that they can only bear it by becoming monuments. The dark folds of their gowns weigh them down and anchor them to earth, while Christ floats free of them. St. John, standing on the right, is no young and beardless youth, but dark-bearded and heavy-set, and he too has become a monument weighed down by the immensity of his grief. Only the centurion dares to look up at the headless Christ, raising his hand in salute, wearing jeweled robes as befitting his rank.

Not only earthquakes have destroyed the living fabric of Nea Moni. There were fires in 1822 and 1828, and there is good reason to believe that robbers have been at work, for here and there a head has vanished, while the rest of the figure remains intact. This is especially noticeable in the mosaic of the Washing of the Feet. Christ in blue and gold stands to the left of a long table, with a white towel round his waist, washing the feet of St. Peter, who looks puzzled and even suspicious, while the rest of the disciples, massed together in garments of blue and coral, watch attentively and fearfully. They are all portraits; the mosaicist is a magnificent portraitist, who knows how to give living expression to features, though the folds of the garments remain stiff and hieratic. So it is with all the surviving mosaics at Nea Moni: the glow of life on the faces, and the convoluted abstract designs of the garments. Christ's towel is the strangest possible shape for a towel, being all wedges and scroll shapes, so that inevitably it becomes something else: a mysterious map, a page from the new Book of the Law, a sudden shock of whiteness against the shimmering gold.

The service was still going on while we gazed at the patchwork of mosaics on the sunlit walls. Once the old priest's voice must have been a magnificent basso profundo, but it quavered now, and sometimes there was only a kind of thin falsetto. There was no congregation, only the priest and the black-robed nuns singing the responses out of key, and from time to time the nuns would turn their heads mischievously to see the strange interlopers who had come to visit them and who spent their time craning at the mosaics. Suddenly the service came to an end. There was no falling off, no preliminary announcement that the end was near. As always in the East song breaks off abruptly, and for a long moment there was silence.

We had expected that the old priest and the nuns would depart and go about their affairs, but instead they gathered around us and pressed small loaves of bread like brown cobblestones into our hands, to celebrate the bread of angels, and led us to the bema where there were more mosaics, including a superb and fiery St. Michael. The candles were snuffed out, and the old priest joked with the nuns. Solemnity had vanished; now there was joy; and you almost expected the priest and the nuns to begin dancing.

One of the nuns, still young, though her skin was burned nearly

black by the sun, saw me admiring the medallion of St. Niketas, one
of the three hermits who found the wonder-working icon.

"Ah, come," she said. "Come and see St. Niketas! He is here,
waiting for you!"

I thought she was mad, for there was a bright gleam in her
eyes.

"Come and see him," she repeated, tugging at my arm, while the
nuns laughed around her and the old priest beamed. "Didn't I tell
you he is here, waiting for you!"

I tried to explain that I knew him well enough from the mosaic
and could not expect to know him better considering that he had
been dead for nearly a thousand years.

She whirled across the church and brought a battered silver
reliquary, which opened to show the top of an ancient skull the
color of rusted iron. She kissed it, crossed herself, offered it to me to
kiss, and all the nuns went off into peals of laughter as they tossed
the reliquary from one to another. They saw no reason to be mutely
reverential. They enjoyed themselves, they were pleased to have St.
Niketas among them, and his familiar presence delighted them. He
had been in his life, if one could trust the mosaic, a severe and
pious hermit. He practiced austerities and lived in a nearby cave.
Now they were making up for the harshness of his life by caressing
him and kissing him and tossing him like a football, until they grew
tired of the game. Then the lid came down over the skull, and they
went out of the church still laughing.

They showed us their treasures, a Byzantine well inlaid with
marble, cavernous and echoing, and a famous refectory table inlaid
with squares of colored marble, but these were small treasures compared with the mosaics on the walls of their church, so small a

church that it could be lost in the aisles of a cathedral. We asked about the wonder-working icon. It had long since vanished. "I have spent sixty years here," the old priest said, "and no one ever asked me about the icon before." We were standing outside the church looking down toward the misty sea and the coasts of Turkey, the cascade of young trees, all the freshness of the earth gleaming in the morning light, and he said kindly: "God be praised, there are so few who come to disturb our peace."

The Throne of Homer

Seven cities claimed to be the birthplace of Homer, but in antiquity the claims of only two cities were taken seriously. They were Smyrna and Chios. Athens, Rhodes, Argos, Colophon and Salamis were the rival contenders, though they never pressed their claims and seemed content only to make the reverential gesture. Chios had the edge over Smyrna, for the *Homeric Hymn to Apollo* speaks of him as "a blind man who dwells in rocky Chios," and we hear of the rhapsodists living on Chios who called themselves the Homeridae and claimed descent from him. Today the village of Khardamyla in the north of the island claims to be the authentic birthplace.

How it came about that Khardamyla, a small village in the foothills of Mount Oros, was able to make so vast a claim is a mystery like everything else connected with Homer. We know the man as little as we know the author of *Genesis*. The portrait bust shows him broad-browed, with a heavy curling beard and a look of godlike calm; almost it might be a portrait of Zeus. These portraits were first made some four hundred years after his death, yet there may be some truth in them. Whatever he looked like, the man was godlike.

Legends were told about him and his life was written down, but the legends and the lives are like echoes of something heard long ago. In *The Contest of Homer and Hesiod* his life ends with a riddle. The poem tells of Homer sitting by the seashore on the island of Ios, watching some boys as they return from fishing.

"Well, my deep-sea fishermen, have you caught anything?" Homer asks them.

"What we caught, we left behind," the boys answer, "and what we are bringing with us we did not catch."

Puzzled, Homer asks them what they mean by this, only to learn that they caught no fish and spent their time catching lice; the lice they caught they left behind, and those they did not catch they carried with them in their clothes. He watched the boys go, and some time later made his way home. On the way he fell in soft earth. It was the beginning of a brief illness, and three days later he was dead. He was buried on the island of Ios, and his epitaph read: "Here the earth covers the holy head of Homer, who celebrated the glory of heroes."

There was a time when I used to think this story was the purest fiction. Now I am not so sure. The life of Homer *must* end on a riddle. The roles *must* be reversed. Instead of telling stories to fishing boys, the boys tell him stories not about heroes, but about the most commonplace of all objects in the Greek world. The story ends with Homer remembering that he had once asked the oracle at Delphi who he was and what country he belonged to, and the oracle answered: "The island of Ios is your mother country and will receive you dead, but beware of the riddle of the young children."

Like so many ghost stories this one has an air of inevitability. The story of the old wandering minstrel is rounded off with a kind of wry tenderness, as Homer dies his very human death.

We hear that note of humanity again in the last verses of the *Homeric Hymn to Apollo*. In old age he sails from Argos, where he was received with extraordinary honors, to the island of Delos where he stands on the altar of horns and delivers the hymn beginning: "I will remember and never forget Apollo the far-shooter." At the end he bids farewell to the maidens:

O maidens, now I bid you farewell,
Calling upon Apollo and Artemis to grant you their blessings.
Remember me. In later years should someone ask you,
A stranger perhaps who has seen and suffered much—
Should he come to the island of Delos and ask you:
"Who was the sweetest singer of them all?
Who made your hearts rejoice most?" tell them:
"A blind man who dwells on rocky Chios was the sweetest singer,
And his poems are the noblest of all, and will endure forever."
Say this, and I shall carry your fame to the ends of the earth
Into the well appointed cities of men,
And they will believe me, for it is no more than the truth.
O never shall I cease to praise Apollo, the far-shooter,
The lord of the silver bow, who was born to the goddess Leto.

Such are the last words of the *Homeric Hymn to Apollo*, written long after Homer was dead. Yet the legend rings true. He must have known Delos well, and as a poet he owed a special worship to

Apollo. It was perhaps inevitable that when he was very old he would sail to Delos and sing a hymn to the god for the last time. Because he was regarded in his lifetime as half divine, no one would have thought it strange that he should stand on the altar of horns, the most sacred place of all.

But all this is legend; Homer vanishes into the bright mists of time. At times we see him in his poems, for a man cannot hide himself completely when he writes twenty-five thousand lines of verse. We see the trencherman, the sailor, the wanderer. There is something of Walt Whitman in him; we see him tending the wounded in the wars and laying out the dead. He has known pirate raids and shipwrecks, suffered hunger and thirst, been captured in war, wandered lonely in a foreign land. He is the stranger who has seen and suffered much, and placed his seeing and suffering at the service of his poetry.

The legends remain. The Chians claim that they possess his throne. Four miles north of the town of Chios along the coastal road, beyond the chromium and plate glass houses of the shipowners, there stands on a rocky outcrop facing the sea a marble throne, once perhaps square, now weathered and pitted by time, and nearly shapeless. Here, according to the legend, he sang his songs under the bare scalded mountains and only a stone's throw away from a running stream now called the Pasha's Fountain. My guidebook says that the white throne had nothing to do with Homer and was probably the altar of some prehistoric church. Poor Homer, to be deprived of his throne!

I confess that I prefer the Chians' version. The setting is so absurdly right. The white rock glitters on a small shelf carved out of the hillside, sounds echo pleasantly, the stream murmurs, the sea lies below. The throne gives the impression of having once been sculptured though all vestiges of sculpture have vanished: it could so easily have been a monumental chair like the carved and ornately beautiful chair of Dionysus which can still be seen in the theater at Athens. That shelf of rock will not hold many people in comfort, perhaps a hundred, but Homer was a court poet and did not demand large audiences. No doubt the princes of Chios lived nearby, as the shipowners do today. The setting is so right that once you have been there, you can scarcely imagine him reciting his poems anywhere else on the island.

So you imagine him climbing the steep path from the seashore, leaning on the arms of a boy, in the heavy sunlight of an ancient summer day. He comes with a small retinue of the *jeunesse dorée* of Chios. Flowers are strewn before him, and more flowers are heaped before his throne, for he loved the smell of fresh flowers and wrote about them often. He wears a laurel wreath, and the shadow of the laurels fall over his blind eyes as he arranges the skirts of his gown and settles on the throne. The rock is spread with carpets, and the princes and princesses of Chios lie at full length on the carpets as though at a feast.

For a long while he says nothing. Long minutes pass while he sits there with his head sunken on his chest. Then quite suddenly the strength seems to pour into him, and at this moment a small lyre is thrust into his hands. He strikes a chord. There, with his back to the mountains and all the sea in front of him, the ships beached below, he sings of the fall of Troy and the wanderings of Odysseus.

The Holy Mountain

AT LESBOS we began to wonder whether we could find a caïque to take us to Mount Athos, which could certainly be considered as an island, for had not Xerxes cut a canal through the isthmus connecting the peninsula with the mainland? We did not like Lesbos. We counted twenty-four million olive trees, wandered over the fortresses built by the Genoese, observed a petrified forest, and came to the conclusion that the island was singularly disappointing. Mytilene resembled Chios. It was not very clean and it was easy to lose oneself in the winding streets left by the Turks. One could lose oneself happily in Myconos or Lindos, and it was the purest pleasure to lose oneself in Rhodes. What we enjoyed most in Lesbos was the sudden flare of red poppies in an olive field along the coast some miles to the east of Mytilene. The days were hot and clammy; the roads were bad; there was no enjoyment in contemplating twenty-four million olive trees. We spoke hopefully of sailing to

Lemnos, and so to Mount Athos, but the harbor was empty of ships. In the end we flew to Athens, and from Athens to Salonica. Then by road to Arnea in the Thracian Chalcidice, and from Arnea to Ierissos on the coast. If there had been an airfield on Mount Athos, it would have been a short flight of one hundred and fifty miles from Mytilene. As it happened, we traveled by plane and car and caïque nearly five hundred miles to reach the Holy Mountain.

Arnea is a lost village high in the hills, and I remember it now for its air of settled melancholy, as of a place where people had suffered so much that they no longer looked to the future. There was one street, a small church, and something that called itself a hotel. The Communists captured the village after the war, and went on to raid Mount Athos; they succeeded in murdering a few monks and looted some treasure, and they held Karyes, the capital of the Athonite communities, for twenty-four hours. They had left a trail of ruin, from which the region has not yet recovered.

A kindly landowner at Arnea offered to write a letter of introduction to the abbot of the monastery of Chilandari, for the formalities are strict and no one can enter the Holy Mountain, which is sovereign territory, without the recommendation of people known to the monks. The landowner knew the monks well, for he bought timber from them, and since he was by nature kindly to excess and the monks were well disposed toward him, his letter of introduction served as a passport wherever we traveled on the mountain, that long slender peninsula which juts out into the Aegean Sea.

"Of course," said the landowner, "they may take an instant dislike to you and order you off their land. One never knows with the monks. They can be very autocratic when they choose."

"Do they choose to be autocratic often?"

"Often," he said, laughing softly as he wandered down the street at dusk, a lonely street where even the shadows seemed to be suffering. "Tomorrow I'll take you to Ierissos. You'll keep in the background while I find a caïque for you. You think Arnea is sad? In Ierissos, too, there were pitched battles with the Communists, and the fighting went on for years. They fought over every inch of these mountains."

We had supper by candlelight in a little wayside inn where the plates were chipped and the tables were bare of all ornament and there was almost no food. The clean wind of the mountains came through the open windows, and the candleflames bent low.

The next morning he drove us down the long winding road to Ierissos, pausing briefly when we came to a gleaming white marble statue looking down over the thickly wooded valleys, the forests stretching as far as the eye could see. He pulled the car to a stop, laughed softly again, and said: "He was born here in this village, and no one thought of remembering him until two years ago, when they put up this statue. He looks like a Roman emperor, and I'm afraid it is a very bad statue."

"Who is it?"

"Aristotle."

Then at a turning of the road came the name of the village: STAGIRA.

There were twelve houses in the village, which was cleaner and more prosperous than Arnea. Here in 384 B.C. Aristotle was born, the son of the physician to the court of the Macedonian king. It was his mother's village, and he spent his early years in the hills, as thickly wooded then as they are now; the shapes of living things and the abstract patterns of growth were his chief delight, and he spent his life studying them. It may have all started with these forests with their different shades of green, lying at the foot of Stagira like a vast abstract painting.

At Ierissos the landowner found us a caïque. For a thousand drachmas they would take us to the monasteries of Chilandari, Iviron, Vatopedi and the Great Lavra. The boatmen would sleep in the caïque, while we slept in the guest-houses. Demetrios was a small ruddy-faced man with a face of old, wrinkled leather, and already his son was beginning to wither in the Aegean sun. They were fishermen and laughed often and sang interminably; and there seemed to be no common ground between their bright laughter and the melancholy of their songs. The caïque was thirty feet long, painted bright red and green, and the paint was peeling away.

As we were about to sail for Chilandari, their women came down to the shore with arms full of flowers. They tossed the flowers into the caïque, laughed, and shouted at the top of their lungs: "Aiyee! Beware of the monks! Be careful! There's no good ever comes from them!"

Vatopedi

Two hours later the caïque sailed into the little harbor of Chilandari, the old Serbian monastery which served as one of the two ports of entry to the sovereign territory of Mount Athos. There was a small house with a balcony hanging over the sea, where an old monk was sunning himself. From the balcony fishing lines drifted into the sea. The monk sat there in a creaking wicker armchair, his eyes very bright under thick curling eyebrows, perfectly content with the world; he had only to pull on his lines, and his dinner would come flying up to him. He was eating from a plate of fish stew, and some of it had slopped over his beard and his stained black gown. He looked mischievous and lazy, and if you met him in the street you would take him for a beggar who did a little thieving on the side.

"Well, yes, they're expecting you at the monastery," he said, and for a moment I thought he must possess second sight or some other mysterious faculty of foreknowledge, for it had not occurred to us that we were expected. He went on: "Your friend telephoned from Ierissos an hour ago. It's all right. Go up to the monastery."

"Where is the monastery?"

"It's a short walk. Five minutes. You couldn't possibly miss it."

He smiled mischievously and went back to his fish stew.

It was not a five-minute walk. Twenty minutes later, after wandering through a forest, we came to the high walls of the monastery. Chilandari means "the thousand," and the name commemorates the thousand monks said to have been massacred beneath its walls during the Iconoclast period. But in the forest and in the fields there was no sign of any monks. Chilandari seemed to be abandoned to an eternal silence. We pulled the gate-bell, and it was five minutes before an old bent white-bearded Russian monk hobbled to the gate and in silence pointed to the wooden steps which climbed three floors to the guest-house. The steps creaked with age, and no wonder, since the monastery was built in the twelfth century. But it was the nineteenth century which met us in the guest-house, where the walls were covered with oleographs of the kings of Serbia, Russia and Montenegro, and to keep them company King Edward VII of England gazed down from the walls through filmy, fly-specked eyes. Turkish coffee was served, and at last another old monk came to greet us, bowing low, and then shaking his sleeves to reveal hands which seemed to have been carved of white alabaster, so delicately clean and transparent they were; and we saw those white alabaster hands wherever we traveled on Mount Athos.

From this guest-room we could look out over the courtyards; swallows kept coming through the open arcades, twittering on the roof beams. Wall clocks chimed the hours with a tinny sound. The furniture was heavy, Victorian, curiously lusterless, as though rarely used. The monastery was huge, and could have held two thousand monks. We asked the guest-master how many monks were in residence. He shook his head sadly.

"There are thirty-six," he said, and there was a long pause before he added: "But only fifteen are active—the rest are old or ill."

"And the fifteen are young?"

"No, the fifteen are old."

He puffed at a cigarette, and gazed out of the windows, as though it were too great an effort to contemplate the time when there would be no more monks at Chilandari. It had been founded in 1197 A.D., and unless a miracle happened, it had only a few more years to live.

"What will happen?" we asked.

"It will survive," he said, but there was no conviction in his voice.

We wandered round the courtyard, admiring the two immense cypresses which may have been as old as the monastery, and the baroque Turkish phiale which resembled an ornate drinking foun-

Monastery of the Great Lavra on Mount Athos.
Wall painting at Vatopedi.
The monks' refectory at the Great Lavra.
Monastery of Nea Moni at Chios.
Courtyard of monastery of Chilandari, Mount Athos.
Surviving column from temple of Hera at Samos.
Temple of Aphaia at Aegina.
Fragment of archaic Apollo at Delos.

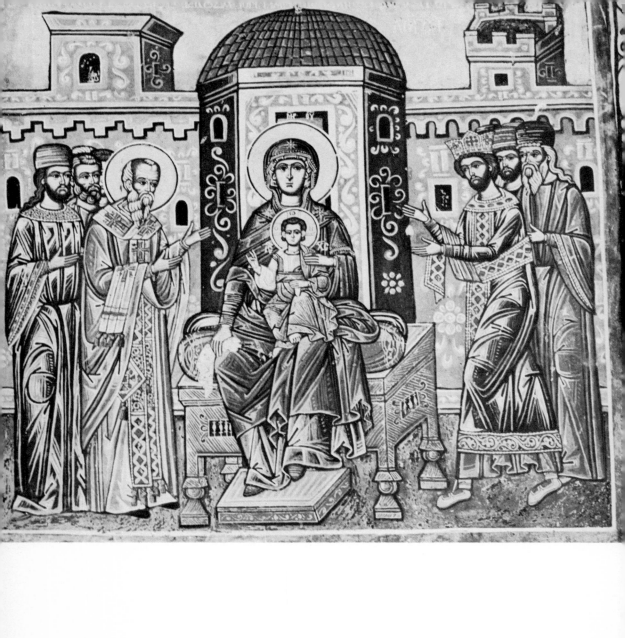

tain, and the huge fortress tower, two hundred feet high, which dominated the monastery, and without admiration we gazed on acres of Macedonian frescoes which would have been wonderful if they had not been repainted in recent times; and in all that time we never saw another monk, and heard no sound, and saw no moving shadows. The guest-master had given us the passport which permitted us to roam freely in the Holy Mountain, and soon we left for Vatopedi, where we knew there would be more than a deaf gatekeeper and a sad-eyed guest-master.

We reached Vatopedi late in the afternoon, and this most venerable of monasteries, founded in the tenth century, surprised us by its resemblance to an enormous beach hotel. A multitude of little balconies, green, red and blue looked down on the sea; there were flowers in the windows; curtains blew in the wind. The façade was painted red. It looked very gay, and we found ourselves wondering whether the orchestra would be playing in the lounge and whether we would be greeted by the maître d'hôtel in a frockcoat with a chrysanthemum in his lapel.

Decidedly the first impression of Vatopedi is one of gaiety; so, too, is the second impression, for we were led by the bushy-bearded guest-master to a salon filled with couches of brocade, and once again there were gilt frames with portraits of the Russian imperial family. There were ormolu lamps, crystal chandeliers, thick blue carpets on the floor. We thought we were in the Ritz Hotel of fifty years ago. The bedroom looked out on the sea.

According to the legend Vatopedi, which means "thorn-bush," commemorates the miraculous finding of Arcadius, the son of Theodosius the Great, in a thornbush on these cliffs; but so early a foundation for the monastery has provoked the theologians into the belief that some other derivation for the name needs to be found. The monks insist that there was an early foundation connected with Arcadius, but they are content to accept that the monastery was founded in 972 A.D. by three brothers from Adrianople, Athanasius, Nicholas, and Antonius. There are many other legends, all of them pointing to the miraculous origin of the monastery. One of these legends is very similar to the legend connected with Tinos. Workmen, digging for the new foundations, uncovered a well and saw a bright light gleaming before a wonder-working icon of the Virgin. They drew up the candle and the icon, and both are preserved in the church, the candle still burning with its unquenchable thousand-year-old light.

The Girdle of the Virgin

The monks of Mount Athos claim to possess a great multitude of treasures, the gifts of mediaeval kings and emperors, kept in mysterious strongboxes which only the most devout are permitted to see and then only on very special occasions. They claim to possess more holy relics than all the rest of Christendom combined, and more great folios in vellum written in Greek than in all the Byzantine libraries in the world. They are proud of their possessions and enjoy displaying them to their rare visitors, while hinting that the most valuable have been and always will be concealed from strangers. At Vatopedi the old librarian carries a great jangling bunch of foot-long keys in the folds of his skirt, and advances toward the library with the air of a conspirator entering forbidden ground. He is the soul of patience and spends three or four minutes inserting one key after another into capacious locks, until at last the library door is open. Then he steps aside, throws up his hands and indicates by the solemnity of his gestures that you are about to see such a library as you will see nowhere else in Europe, for Vatopedi is quite easily the richest of all the Athonite monasteries, possessing more manuscripts and more jeweled chalices and relics than the others, and being the envy of them all.

But when you enter the library, set high up on the monastery wall, there is only a very small room with perhaps a hundred books and a few pages of parchment inscribed in heavy purple ink with the signatures of Byzantine emperors racing across the bottom of the page. These signatures are faintly alarming. The lettering is square, deliberate and powerful; the august voice of the emperor still echoes. These bulls were written when the Byzantine empire was reduced to the size of a principality and when the Turks were at the gates, but the emperors wrote as though all eastern Europe belonged to them. In a glass case there is a single page from a codex of the Gospel of St. John, the black ink looking so fresh on the page that it might have been written this very morning. "It is the earliest known," the librarian announces with pardonable pride. "It was written in the fifth century." It is not the earliest known, for the sands of Egypt have produced papyri with fragments of the Gospel at least two centuries earlier, but this is a small matter, not worth arguing about. He waves his hand toward the shelves where the folios in their pigskin bindings repose peacefully. "There is no greater collection of Byzantine manuscripts anywhere," he intones, although the Bibliothèque Nationale and Dumbarton Oaks between them have perhaps ten times as many. So he goes about the small room, pulling occasional manuscripts from the shelves, always a little breathless and with a puzzled expression, as though he could not bring himself to believe that anything was to be gained by disturbing their peace.

There was, however, one object in the room which was curiously appealing. It was not a great work of art, and could not compare with Byzantine mosaics and ivories which can be found in large numbers outside Mount Athos. It was an impudent and revealing work, and very memorable, because it admirably conveyed the strength and weakness of the declining empire, being at once fierce and delicate, wonderfully and exactly proportioned and altogether too ornamental. It was a cup ten inches high, but what a cup! No one would ever dream of drinking out of it. No lips had ever touched it, and no wine would ever be poured into it. It was perfectly appropriate that it should stand in a glass case in a small musty library in an ancient monastery.

The shallow bowl of gold-flecked jasper was supported on a silver-gilt stalk of a kind that would be appropriate in a short candlestick, being octagonal with an octagonal base. Halfway down the candlestick there was an octagonal boss, from which two slender and minuscule dragons reared up to form handles. You know they are dragons, because they are winged, but they resemble very small lizards. These lizards are very thin and look famished; they also look powerful. They grip the edges of the jasper cup with their tiny claws, little devils made of whipcord and sprung metal, with so much violence in them that they seem to be still quivering and biting into the cup. They represent a tradition which is very old, for among the treasures found at Mokhlos in Crete there is a small steatite lid which has for handle a lean hunting dog which also resembles a lizard, and is bent and stretched out in the same way. The hunting dog from Mokhlos can be dated about 1500 B.C. The jasper cup must belong to some date between 1350 and 1380 A.D., for the bold inscription at the base informs us that it was presented by Manuel Cantacuzene, despot of Mistra, who reigned during that period. He was the son of the brilliant Emperor John VI Cantacuzene, who usurped the throne and plunged the Byzantine empire into civil war until at last he was forced to abdicate; and from being an emperor robed in purple he became the monk Ioasaph robed in a black gown at Vatopedi.

Sometimes a very small object can illuminate a whole century, and this cup which belongs to its time and has almost no relevance to our own, is just such an object. It is so small a thing that on entering that cluttered library, it would be easy to miss it. Once seen, it becomes a monument.

There is power in it, but it is the power of a declining empire; there is ingenuity, but it is the ingenuity of desperation; it is exquisitely shaped and balanced, and wrought with intricate care and affection, but it serves no other purpose than to bring glory to the giver. It was made to be remembered. Even now I can remember the exact shape of the shallow bowl with the gold-flecked waving patterns of russet and sea-green, and the glint of gold, and the way the bronze dragons snapped their teeth into the rim of the bowl.

We asked whether we could photograph the cup, but the librarian shook his head. Such treasures were not to be defiled by photography unless special permission had been obtained from Karyes, and this, we understood, would be granted only with the permission and consent of the Greek foreign office. How long would it take to acquire all the necessary permits? Perhaps three or four weeks. It was the same wherever we traveled in Greece; the whims of the curators were like the peace of God, beyond all understanding. Permission to photograph minor objects would be categorically refused, while rare and valuable objects, which we scarcely dared to ask for, would be placed at our disposal. Thus, though the jasper cup was refused to us, we were told we could photograph anything we liked in the church.

The church was a jewel-box with so many gilded pendants and golden chandeliers and giant candlesticks and silver icons and brilliantly colored frescoes that at first it had the effect of a beautiful and brightly lit aquarium, for the gold light flowed in waves. Light flashed from the heavy circular candelabra hanging from the roof, which must have been twenty feet in diameter with some twenty yard-long candles rising from it, and from the golden haloes of innumerable saints, and from the Pantocrator who gazed down from the gold heavens in the dome, and these gold lights did not remain still, but darted continually from wall to wall. It was not a very large church, and there was no single object which was wrought masterfully, for there were no great and memorable mosaics, no finely painted frescoes, but the whole flashed, flared and frolicked with Byzantine exuberance. There was something childish in that massive display of jeweled ornamentation, and yet it was oddly satisfying. There was the sense of a calculated splendor, of a deliberate striving toward the utmost magnificence in a small space. Of all the buildings we saw on the Holy Mountain this church was the most captivating.

The red-bearded monk with the manners of a court chamberlain led us behind the iconostasis to the small sacristy where the most sacred objects were kept. He lit a candle, crossed himself, and then proceeded to display the treasures. There was a piece of the True Cross, the skull of St. Gregory the Theologian, and a finger of John the Baptist, all in their jeweled reliquaries. But the most precious object, enclosed in a large silver and enamel box, was the girdle of the Virgin presented to the monastery in the fourteenth century by King Lazar I of Serbia. What could be seen of the girdle was no more than six or seven inches of reddish camel-hair set in a silver groove across the middle of the box.

Many relics of the Virgin have survived, and there are still churches in northern Italy which preserve vials of her milk and of her tears. Her wedding-ring is in Perugia, her veil in Chartres. This little strand of dyed camel-hair is perhaps no more authentic than the others, but it has the virtue of simplicity and even of humility. The red-bearded monk pulled numerous skulls from the cupboard, reciting a litany of the saints over the dull and tarnished reliquaries, and left us unmoved. The girdle in the little jewel-box was more impressive because it was so small, so worn with age, so slender. It was almost dust. It was inconceivable that it had ever belonged to the Virgin, but it seemed to exist in its own right; and in its frailty it was venerable.

The Great Lavra

We sailed along the coast of the Holy Mountain hoping to come across a monastery which had the look of holiness, and instead saw splendid hotels perched on cliffs or battlemented fortresses or country estates set among forests of pines. The Great Lavra alone appeared from the sea to have the appearance of great age, and certainly it was the most beautiful, the most unkempt, and the most tragic. The fortress-like building could hold an army of monks, and we saw perhaps twenty in all the time we spent there.

The Great Lavra has a small rocky harbor, and as we sailed into the harbor we saw a truck laden with tins of kerosene about to make the long climb to the monastery. We were so surprised to see a truck there that we almost forgot to hail the bearded driver. Just in time we managed to clamber on the back of the truck, and so made our way triumphantly to the monastery gate. Beyond the Great Lavra the huge ash-white shoulder of Mount Athos rose in the clear skies.

The Great Lavra is the senior house on the peninsula, having been founded by Athanasius of Trebizond in 963 A.D. He was one of those unruly monks who are a prey to demons, and he fought them vigorously with his iron-tipped staff during all the years he spent on the Holy Mountain. Once the demons broke his ankle to spite him; he roared like thunder, whirled the iron-tipped staff around his head, and sent them away howling. The young Nicephoros Phocas, soon to become emperor, became his friend, and on a visit to the mountain before invading Crete he rejoiced to receive the blessing of Athanasius, promising in return that he would take the vows. Having conquered Crete, he forgot his vows, stormed into Byzantium and seized the throne. When he was murdered by John Tzimiskes, Athanasius seems to have been quietly content. Nicephoros Phocas had endowed his monastery; John Tzimiskes endowed it with even greater wealth; and in the church a fresco depicting the murdered emperor charmingly confronts a fresco depicting his assassin. The stormy life of Athanasius ended when he fell from the scaffolding while attempting to raise the dome of the church; the dome collapsed; and the saint with four workmen were crushed to death by the debris. His small dark tomb lies beside the chapel screen. There, too, lies his iron-tipped staff and the iron collar he wore as an act of occasional penance.

The severity of Athanasius himself is stamped on the brooding church, for the church is a simple one, though crowded with frescoes. We attended the interminable night service, while the monks chanted and moved in the half-darkness like stealthy ghosts, vanishing behind the iconostasis and then appearing again, looking more grey and ashen than before; and it was a relief when the sun came up and the dew sparkled on the grass growing wild in the courtyards. I remember the shoddy guest-rooms, and the gaudy little museum, and the skull of St. Basil wearing a silver crown, and the skull of John the Baptist in a battered reliquary, but I remember with more affection the view of the battlemented monastery from above as the sun was setting, while the monks rhythmically scythed the long grass.

A Strange Monk

All morning the fat monk with the silky beard had been following us as we wandered around the monastery. Whenever we took photographs he was watching, and when we hurried along the cobbled road leading from one courtyard to another, hoping to avoid him, we would find him waiting for us. He seemed to have some sixth sense and knew where we would go, even when we did not know ourselves. He had a sweet and sickly smile, and he was always fingering his beard.

We could make nothing of him, for he was usually silent. We knew him by the rustle of his skirts and by the white face which hovered permanently in the background; there was something malevolent about him like the malevolence of a cruel child. Once, indeed, near the refectory of the monks, he stopped me to remind me that it was unseemly to walk on holy ground with my hands in my pockets, and he went on to explain that the entire monastery had been consecrated and therefore we were on holy ground wherever we walked. "God walks here," he said, and seemed pleased with himself. Then he dismissed me with a wave of his hand. His fingers were plump and carefully manicured.

He rarely spoke to us, and we had the feeling that he regarded us as inferior creatures, not worthy of conversation. Through him, God held a watching brief for our behavior. We had obtained permission to photograph in the church, but as soon as Alexander set up his cameras he appeared again and told us it was strictly forbidden. We asked who had forbidden it, and he said he had the authority to forbid it; but in fact he had no authority, and we went on photographing. What was particularly galling to Alexander, who had to translate for my benefit everything he said, was that he spoke in the precise, mincing tones of an Athenian aristocrat. In just such a voice a court chamberlain might address some minion from the scullery.

There was no escape from him, for he had attached himself to us, and soon we came to accept him as part of the scenery. He was like the sky, all-pervading, and if for a moment he vanished, it was like a cloud covering the sun. His white bubble of a face continually haunted us.

Once when he had vanished for a few moments, I said: "I don't believe he exists."

We looked around, and there was no sign of him.

"He has probably gone to lunch," Alexander said, breathing a sigh of relief, "or perhaps he has simply given up the chase."

"I think he wants something?" I suggested.

"What on earth could he want?"

"Probably a tip."

"No, he is a monk. He wouldn't accept a tip from us. He probably has nothing else to do, and he is bored, and it amuses him to watch us."

I said testily: "If he has nothing better to do, he should go into the church and say his prayers."

"He has been saying them all night," Alexander said. "He does not have to say them all day. Poor fellow, he probably wants some companionship."

We could not forget him. There was something strangely familiar about him. We both had the feeling that we had met him before. He had thick red lips, and his beard was jet black and oily and glinted in the sun. The mincing walk, too, was familiar. Even the voice reminded us of someone we had known, though, try as we might, we were never able to place him. So he followed us, strangely evil, vanishing only to reappear around the next corner, so much like a restless ghost that we imagined he was perhaps a revenant, long dead, but permitted to return to earth for a brief while. "If you put out your hand," Alexander said, "there would be nothing there."

Wearying of the strange monk, we attached ourselves to another

monk, a small gnome-like man with a long beard who led us into
the Great Refectory, now used by the monks only on ceremonial
occasions, with its rows of painted saints with glowing haloes on the
walls and two parallel rows of horseshoe-shaped tables of blue
stone. It was the most pleasant of all the rooms in the Great Lavra,
filled with light and color and air, very restful. Above the martial
rows of saints were more frescoes, reaching to the wooden roof.
The blessed marched in stately columns of gold and scarlet, while
the damned writhed in black and midnight blue. Yet the effect was
one of rainbow-colored quietness, as though the walls were heaped
with flowers.

The gnome-like monk sat at one of the blue tables, scarcely
bothering to watch us. He permitted flashlight by simply nodding
his head when the flash was shown to him. The Great Refectory, he
told us, had been much photographed, and to help photographers
the Great Lavra had installed floodlamps near the ceiling. Regretfully the diesel engine supplying electricity to the monastery was
out of order. It was hoped that an electrician from Salonica would
repair it, but only God in His infinite wisdom knew when the electrician would come.

The gnome sat there very quietly, nodding his head a little, interested and disinterested, not really caring. Sometimes he would
look down at his hands, which were heavily veined, and sometimes
he would gaze absentmindedly at the rows of saints as though half-
wondering what they were doing there. Pigeons flew through the
open windows and settled on the roof beams, and once a black
tomcat marched up the whole length of the painted hall, having
heard the cooing of the pigeons.

An hour passed while Alexander took photographs, and still the
gnome-like monk sat there in brooding patience. He never smiled,

never by even a gesture suggested impatience or displeasure; and when at last Alexander put his equipment away, he rose, made the faintest of bows, and slipped out of the refectory.

"I think he is a very lowly member of the community," Alexander said. "I think he is a cook. Anyway, he is much better than old Poke Fingers."

"Who is Poke Fingers?"

"The one who followed us all morning. Always poking his fingers into his beard. He's gone now. Probably taking a siesta."

He laughed and shrugged his shoulders. We were well rid of the specter who haunted us all morning and could breathe freely again.

There was a great porphyry bowl at the entrance to the church, and Alexander decided to photograph it. The bowl stood in a little painted kiosk. It was cracked, but could still hold water and every month it was used for the preparation of holy water. The dome of the kiosk was reputed to belong to the eleventh century, but all the painting was new, very bright, and wonderfully inconsequential. It was a gay little kiosk and the porphyry bowl reflected the colors of the dome.

He had been photographing for five minutes when we became aware of the monk with the silky beard. It was something one felt on the nerves and in the air, for there was no sign of him in the courtyard which lies between the church and the refectory unless he was hiding behind the giant cypresses. I wandered out of the kiosk, leaving Alexander at his work, and went round the church and came back again, but he was nowhere in sight.

"Did you see him?" Alexander asked.

"No, but I am convinced he hasn't gone very far. He is somewhere around."

"Damn right you are. He is probably looking through some shutters. I get a feeling that he is crawling down my neck. I don't know what he is up to, and I don't care."

The truth was that we did care, and cared very deeply. The air seemed to be charged with menace. It was not hatred or horror: it was simply that the man's presence was completely unnerving. It was as though he possessed some strange power to cast a spell over us, and wherever he was, the air seemed suddenly lifeless. We decided to leave the Great Lavra. We had attended the night service, seen the treasures, talked to the abbot, photographed as many buildings as we were permitted to photograph, and we wanted to get away. We would return to Ierissos and make our way somehow to Thasos, and it would be good to get back to the islands again.

"So it's all settled?" Alexander said. "We go now?"

"Yes, we go now."

We put the camera equipment away. We decided to go back to the dormitory and get everything ready for the journey to Ierissos. We had hardly stepped out of the kiosk when Alexander stopped dead in his tracks and pointed to a high balcony overlooking the courtyard. The monk with the silky beard was leaning over the balcony rail. He had been watching us all the time.

We packed our bags and sent word to the men on the caïque that we were ready to leave for Ierissos. It was very peaceful in the dormitory. The German alpinist had vanished, having decided not to climb Mount Athos but to walk to Karyes, the seat of the government of the Holy Mountain, a few miles away. For a few moments we gazed down at the sea far below with a sense of loss and disillusionment, in a mood which was not anger but akin to anger. No doubt there were good monks on Mount Athos, but we never saw them. We saw pride and despair, riches amid poverty, the corroding emptiness of the place. The monks sometimes wondered why the young did not come to replenish the stock of novices, and they would speak nervously of what would happen in ten or twenty years' time. For a thousand years monks had continued to live on the mountain, obeying laws first instituted in the reign of Constantine IX Monomachus, offering masses and attending to the liturgies, reciting their endless prayers, and now at last by ceaseless repetition even their prayers had come to lose their meaning.

"What will happen when there are only ten monks left on the mountain?" I asked.

"The Greek government will have to step in," Alexander said. "There doesn't seem to be any other way. Now there are monasteries with ten or fifteen active members where once there were more than a thousand, and already the numbers are below the irreducible minimum. They have wealth from the timber. They can afford to hire labor. Each monastery is a little feudal estate, and the time for feudal estates has gone. So eventually the Holy Mountain will become a national possession. There's no hope for it. The community of monks is dying, and the process of putrefaction has set in. It's all dead—dead—dead—"

We were still talking about the death that hovered over the Holy Mountain when the monk with the silky beard stepped into the dormitory. For a fleeting moment we thought he had come to arrest us. He stood by the door, smiling his smile of authority, the fingers of his left hand threading through the luxuriant and glistening beard. Suddenly he beckoned us. It was an imperious beckoning, with a great flapping of the black sleeves, but we refused to answer his summons. We were sitting by the window, the whole length of the dormitory away, and we were in no mood to meet him in the shadowy region near the door. He looked tense and excited, and there was something satanic about him.

"Come," he said, but we did not come.

As though in a fury he marched up to the windows, making impatient snapping sounds with his fingers. He knew how to manipulate his sleeves with telling effect, and he sailed across the room like a black-sailed ship. He sat down on the edge of an unmade bed, arranged the folds of his gown, and said: "Forgive me, if I ask for your names and addresses." His small pencil was poised over a leather-bound notebook. "Ah, so you are both Americans? So you will tell Americans about all you have seen on Mount Athos, yes? There are no sanctuaries like this in America, are there? Of course, you will never find anything else in the world like the monasteries. We have great treasures here. Sanctity is here. God walks here. We never demand anything from the rest of the world for all our ceaseless prayers."

So he went on, gazing down at his hands, tapping nervously with his pencil on the notebook, and sometimes flinging out his sleeves to ease the soft pressure on his wrists. For another five minutes he celebrated the heroic sanctity of Mount Athos, where alone there was sanity in a tormented world, but we knew he had not come to tell us these things. At last the face seemed to crumple and the hands began to move more impatiently through the beard, as he said: "Have you any cigarettes, any sugar?" His voice was cracked. He was almost screaming. In one pocket I had a full pack of cigarettes, in the other there was a pack with only a solitary cigarette. I gave him the pack with the solitary cigarette.

"Is that all you have?" he asked.

We nodded.

"No sugar?"

We said nothing. He looked so helpless sitting there, staring out to sea. He puffed on the cigarette yearningly, absorbing all the smoke, breathing deeply, the fight gone out of him. All morning he had been a figure of authority and menace, but now he was like a child yearning for another candy. We watched him without pity, as one might watch a dying snake. He finished the cigarette, flung it out of the window, and said: "Haven't you got just one more?"

We walked out of the dormitory in silence. At the door we paused and looked back. He was staring after us, and there was a wild light in his eyes, and he was fingering his beard.

Thasos

WE COASTED along the shore for about half an hour until we came to the monastery of Philotheos, red-roofed and turreted, looking from the sea like a large farmhouse high up on the jutting rocks. The monk Gregorios had some business there, and he had asked us to put in at the monastery. He had red hair and a pleasant freckled face, and what was chiefly noticeable about him was that he walked like a sailor and seemed uncomfortable in his ragged gown.

We asked him how long he had been a monk, and at first he shrugged his shoulders. He was not a man of many words. He spoke slowly and hesitantly—about the war which had turned his thoughts to religion, and about the wife who had abandoned him and turned his thoughts to the monastic life. He had three children, and they were being looked after by foster parents. He was glad to be free of the world, but he borrowed our cigarettes and spoke of the world regretfully. He had spent five years at the Great Lavra, and was now about to spend six months at Philotheos.

"And after that?"

"I shall go back to Great Lavra."

"And you'll never come back to the world?"

"Never," he said, and a little later: "It is hard on the mountain, unbelievably hard. When I am a little older, I may come back to the world."

"Are there many who come back to the world?"

"Not many—four or five a year. Especially the young monks, and that is why you see very few of them. The mountain is dying." He went on a little later: "It is not the discipline, or even the loneliness. The mountain is changing. We do not know what will happen to it. A hundred years ago it must have been much easier to be a monk."

He looked troubled and lost as he sat in the stern of the caïque. He was a tall man, well built, with a spiky red beard, and at a distance you would take him for a man who was physically and spiritually strong, but at close quarters he gave an impression of weakness and indecision, as though at every moment of the day he scarcely knew what he was doing. He invited us to visit Philotheos, where there was a wonder-working icon of Our Lady of Tenderness, but instead we decided to strike out for the island of Thasos. The truth was that we were weary of the monasteries and all their works. The last we saw of him he was climbing up the steep steps to the monastery with his heavy pack on his back, taking the steps two at a time.

So we left the small rocky inlet and made for the open sea without regret, feeling free again—free of the ghosts and the vast pretensions of holiness and the monks who moved like dolls jerked by invisible strings. We had seen four monasteries and lost many illusions. We had thought that in some mysterious way Byzantium survived; we had imagined faces of the purest sanctity and great works of art, but there was more sanctity in the face of a Greek peasant boy than in any of the monks we saw, and there were more great works of art in the Byzantine museums than in the monasteries. Mount Athos was dying its slow death, already frozen into a gesture of immobility; and in its dying it was unlamented.

From the sea the Holy Mountain gradually became a smudge of green on the horizon as one by one the monasteries vanished among the trees, first Philotheos, then Iviron, then Karyes high up on a shoulder of the hills. Finally the blue cone of Mount Athos itself vanished in a wreath of smoking clouds. The sailors were laughing, glad to be free of the brooding menace of the monasteries. About half an hour after we left Philotheos they began singing.

Though a small *meltemi* had been blowing earlier in the day, the seas were now calm and silvery grey under the grey clouds which seemed to spring up from nowhere until the whole sky was covered with them. One can be burned black in summer in a half-day of crossing the Aegean in an open caïque, and so we were delighted by the clouds which kept the sun at bay. Alexander was worried. He had the photographer's particular dislike of clouds, and imagined that all Greece was now shadowless. When we came close to Thasos the clouds miraculously lifted, and he smiled again.

Demetrios sat crosslegged on his small engine-house with the rudder rope between his knees, chanting his endless songs which were like the songs a baby chants to itself, for there were no words, only sounds, and the pitch would rise if there came a spluttering from the engine-room and then he would shout out some order to the boy, and resume his wordless chanting. It pleased him that we were going to Thasos, for that meant another thousand drachmas in his purse, and with luck and a following wind he would be in Ierissos that night. In the shadowless light, under the grey clouds, he looked very old with his red leathery skin twisted into a multitude of wrinkles. He was thirty-five, but the sun had sucked so much juice from his face that he might have been seventy.

Even from a distance Thasos looked pleasantly inviting, green and lush, with softly curving mountains. The sky was now a soft pearly blue as the clouds melted away, and in this light the mountains had the look of being freshly sculptured, youthful, graceful, and not in the least ferocious, as we had been led to expect from the guidebooks, which insisted that Thasos had the wild aspect of neighboring Thrace. From the beginning, when we landed at the little seaport at Maries, what impressed us most was the beauty of the mountains of Thasos, which could be compared only with the mountains of Chios for sheer nobility of outline and soaring exuberance. The Chian mountains are gaunt and stark, being bare bone with no skin on them, and they are far more massive, masculine and vigorous. The mountains of Thasos are feminine and spirited and gracefully curved, with the power flowing through them.

So it happened that we would find ourselves gazing at the mountains of Thasos with the same feeling with which one gazes at works of art, wondering how they had come into existence. We never saw one mountain which was displeasing. In some miraculous way these green slopes appeared to possess a life of their own. They are the only mountains I have ever seen which looked as though at any moment they might begin to skip and leap.

Demetrios was singing louder than ever as we put into Maries. It was a pleasant fishing village, with whitewashed houses gathered around a blue bay, holding the sun in its arms. No one seemed to know the origin of the name; it might have been named after Mary by the Crusaders, or from a Greek word meaning "blackberries." Tourists rarely came there. The people made a living from fishing, kept beehives and tended their olive fields. Demetrios spread out his hands; he had brought us to the island, and now he was ready to depart. He explained that it was too late for him to reach the port of Thasos before night fell, we would find a taxi easily, and in twenty minutes we would reach the island capital. Singing more loudly than ever, he jumped into the caïque and sailed for Ierissos.

We were to learn later that Maries possesses only one broken-down taxi and even a Rolls Royce could not have made the journey to the port of Thasos in less than half an hour. We heard that the taxi was being repaired, and then that it was in some other part of the island, and then that it had been dismantled; and over ham sandwiches on the quay-side, we saw much shaking of heads. We said we would walk to Thasos, and they burst out laughing. They laughed still louder when they heard that Demetrios said that Thasos was only twenty minutes away. We resigned ourselves to spending the night at Maries, where the quays were made of snow-white marble. Two white kittens floated in the bay, while their mother prowled in search of them, mewing plaintively. A ten-year-old boy with patched trousers, who looked as though he had stepped out of one of the Acropolis marbles, danced on the marble shore for no better reason than that he had nothing else to do, while the sun sank slowly over Mount Athos far in the distance and Demetrios in his caïque became no more than a speck on the golden sea. There were no other ships in sight, until a lone fisherman paddled into the harbor with the day's catch of three silver sardines.

So an hour passed, while messengers went in search of the taxi, which was reported to be in three different places, and the Salonica radio blared out the latest dance tunes, and the boy from the Acropolis marbles kicked up his heels. The shadows lengthened, the red roofs on the other side of the bay took on a darker color, and soon Maries would settle down for the night. It was already growing dark when the taxi arrived. It was in one piece, though the driver looked as though he had spent the intervening hour putting the taxi together. His price for driving to Thasos was five hundred drachmas. He admitted that it was an exorbitant price, and explained that every journey to Thasos reduced the value of his taxi, for the roads were bad—very bad indeed.

We thought he was exaggerating until, a mile from Maries, we encountered a road like the giant's causeway, so rock-strewn that it seemed impossible for any car to survive the punishment. We jumped and jerked our way to Thasos, while the driver tested our nerves by gesticulating with both hands as he denounced the government in Athens for doing so little for the upkeep of the island roads. The taxi's entrails shuddered and clanked, and from time to time small pieces of the taxi fell away and went bouncing along the road. I was sitting in the back, and begged him to drive more carefully. He turned right about and barked that no one had ever dared to call him a careless driver; he had a wife he loved and four children he adored, and he was therefore not a man who could be accused of carelessness on the road. I took what comfort I could by gazing at the endless rows of gnarled olive trees which were as beautifully sculptured as the mountains.

When we reached Thasos it was dark, and there was almost no town. There were two hotels, five or six streets, and a marine promenade a quarter of a mile long made of the purest marble. We were to learn the next day that the town was so small that you could almost put it in the palm of your hand, and so quiet at noon that you could almost imagine that the inhabitants would never wake from their siesta. There was the scent of pine and mint, and darkness everywhere. Thasos was already going to sleep.

The Fields of Ruins

In ancient days the island was famous for its gold mines, its marble fortress and harbor, and its checkered history. Its coins were stamped with a kneeling satyr bearing on his lap a nymph who was clearly to be shown no mercy; nor was any mercy shown to the islanders. Thasos changed hands six times during the war between Athens and Sparta. It was always being pillaged or raided, because it lies on the sea-road between Athens and the Black Sea, and between Asia Minor and Thrace, where there were even richer gold mines. Violence seems to have been a way of life on the island, which produced one great painter, one great poet, and the most formidable of all Greek athletes.

The name of the athlete was Theagenes, and it was related of him that at the age of nine, when returning from school he tore off from its base one of the statues in the market place, threw it over his shoulders and carried it home. The people decided to kill him for this act of impiety toward the god, but an old and venerable man urged that he should simply be punished by being made to put the statue back again; a boy so strong would bring great merit to the city. So it happened, for he went on to become a prize athlete, winning nearly all the contests he entered. Before he died he accumulated 1,400 crowns. He was especially famous for his victories in the pancration, but he was also famous as a runner. When he died, one of his enemies came every night to his bronze statue which stood in the market place, and gave it a good whipping. One night the statue grew weary of the man's insolence, fell to the ground and crushed the man who had so thoughtlessly hoped to punish a dead athlete. The man's relatives brought the matter to court. It was decided that the statue was dangerous and should therefore be banished following the Draconian law that even inanimate objects must be banished when they cause mortal harm. Accordingly the statue was pitched into the sea.

The adventures of the statue were not yet over, for soon the whole island suffered from a drought and envoys were sent to the oracle at Delphi to ask what should be done to avoid starvation. Apollo answered: "Remember the great Theagenes." So the city fathers gave orders that the statue should be dredged up and once more placed in a position of honor in the market place. Theagenes became an immortal god to whom sacrifices were offered, and his statue was worshipped in places far from Thasos. Like Apollo himself, he healed the sick and protected athletes.

Archilochos was one of the first settlers of Thasos, and the Greeks regarded him as the greatest of their poets after Homer, for he was believed to be the inventor of the iambic line. Horace said of him that he armed himself with the iambic "out of rage." He was a man who hated lustily, and the scattered fragments of his surviving works suggest that he raged with a pure and devout passion, most of all raging against himself. Of Thasos he wrote: "This wheatless island is like a donkey's spine, bristling with a tangle of wild woodland," and he went on to compare it unfavorably with his native Paros which he had formerly dismissed as a land with nothing but figs and fish. He was the son of an aristocrat and a slave woman, and he wrote with brutal force as well as nobility. He fought in the wars, and once threw his shield away and ran, celebrating the event later in a poem which has been discussed by generations of critics as an avowal of cowardice, whereas it was more probably an ironic commentary on all warriors everywhere; and at last returning to Paros he was killed in battle by a native of Naxos. Like Homer he was an islander, and since he spent a good deal of his short life carousing in Thasos, the Thasians quite properly regard him as one of their own.

There was violence, too, in Polygnotos, the third of the great Thasians, the most famous painter of his time. In the assembly room of the Cnidians at Delphi he painted two great wall paintings, one on the fall of Troy and the other on Odysseus' visit to Hades. He was the first among the Greeks to depict violent human emotions on the faces of the heroes, and these paintings gave him every opportunity to depict the heroes in their agony. He seems to have been the first of all known painters to employ perspective, and Aristotle described him as the most ethical of men because he sought after psychological truth. The great wall paintings at Delphi probably resembled Michelangelo's wall painting in the Sistine Chapel with crowds of jostling figures in irregular tiers. Unlike Michelangelo he was careful to inscribe the names of the heroes he depicted on his paintings with the result that Pausanias, coming to Delphi six centuries later, was able to describe them so minutely

that it became possible for scholars to reconstruct them. The paintings survived for another two hundred years, and then vanished
from sight. Polygnotos also painted battle scenes, and in these too
he gloried in violence.

But on that summer morning there were no signs of violence in
sleepy Thasos. The scarlet boats were beached, the fishermen were
mending their nets, and the agora built in honor of Zeus Agoraios,
protector of civil concord, was being used for the most peaceful of
occupations—it had become a haying field, the bright hay lying
among the broken columns. The scent of pines drifted down from
the high mountain behind the village, and the scent of enormous
roses mingled with the hay.

It was an enchanting place, perhaps because it was strangely
empty and so gave the impression of still belonging to the ancient
Greeks. The ancient mole lay below the surface of the sea; huge
marble walls were still in place; and coming across plowed fields
you would find yourself face to face with one of the ancient marble
gates. Satyrs were evidently worshipped in Thasos, for one of the
gates carries a relief showing a naked satyr with a member two feet
long dancing and clasping a drinking cup, while a hundred yards
away, set in an olive grove is the gate of Zeus with another relief
showing Zeus standing before Eileithyia, and though the relief has
weathered, it seems to represent the birth of Dionysus, one of the
guardian gods of the ancient city. So everywhere, at a street corner
or along the beach, the ancient Greeks meet you. The whole village
has become a museum. Once a hundred thousand men lived in this
seaport city. Now in the whole island there are only eighteen thousand.

Best of all, perhaps, is the theater which stands halfway up the steep hill in the shadow of the pines, overlooking the sea. The half-circle of marble seats is dappled with leaves. It is a place to linger in, in the pine-scented shade, with the yellow beach below and the dark submarine shape of the ancient mole curving out to sea. All is bright outside, but the stage is dark and the seats vanish into obscurity. Not far away is a sunlit bay with neither a house nor a ship in sight; there is only the bay, with the pines leaning against the wind.

Once, at the bottom of the hill, Alexander looked down and saw something green glinting at his feet. It was a small copper coin washed down by the winter rains, dating perhaps from Roman times. He looked for others, but there were no more to be seen.

The museum is small, set in a pleasant rose garden, and has one treasure possessed by no other museum in the world. This is a huge archaic Apollo nearly twelve feet high, excavated from the wall of the acropolis where no doubt it had been placed at a time of war to strengthen the defenses of the city. The statue is unfinished, rudely carved. It is not as large as the Apollo which once stood at Delos, but it is the largest and most monumental of all the surviving Apollos. He holds a ram against his breast, signifying that he is Apollo Karnaios, the protector of flocks; but the ram is scarcely more than an abstract design. Apollo stands there in towering majesty, one arm at his side, the other holding the ram, and the delicate curls fall over his shoulders—the sculptor has evidently enjoyed the intricate play of these curls, leaving the carving of the face to the last. So, too, with the kouros on the island of Naxos— the face was an egg, uncarved, untouched, left to the last. Even unfinished, the statue has energy and power, striding forward with an appearance of imperious ease; and the museum seems too small to hold it.

There is a pretty head of Dionysus in the museum, and a few bits and pieces of no particular worth or beauty, but it is the Apollo twelve feet high which holds the attention. The grey and weathered stone looms in the doorway above the rose garden, dark and shadowy. It would look better in the agora in the sunlight, amid the fresh-mown hay.

Poros

IN THE GLARE of noonday the candy-seller pushed his cart along the waterfront. It was a glass-walled cart with trays of pistachio nuts, loukoumi and spun candy. They were inviting trays, pink and green and gold, but no one paid any attention to them except two children who, after much debating among themselves, decided to buy a few pistachio nuts. Then they vanished, and the old candy-seller was left alone. There was a black monkey on the roof of the cart, and sometimes he would pull a string, and the wooden monkey would squeak and wave its arms and legs, but as the time passed he pulled the string less often. By one o'clock there was no one left on the waterfront. The shops were closed, the restaurants were silent. Poros slept its long sleep.

So it happened day after day in the summer—the heavy drugged sleep of Poros which began about noon and continued until mid-afternoon. Athenians come to Poros to sleep, and the foreigners

soon fall into the habit. Businessmen come here to take the cure—
the cure is sleep. Poros, they will tell you, is the most restful of all
the islands in the Aegean. In summer they come in their thousands,
paying exorbitant rents for small cell-like rooms in the crowded
town which climbs up and down a small mountain facing the
Peloponnesian coast. The town has no history and almost no name;
the word *poros* means "the straits," and more properly applies to
the stretch of water which flows between the island and Galata,
with its forests of lemon trees. Poros has been described as a flock
of seagulls feeding on a rock, and it is true that the great cluster of
white and pink houses forming a kind of pyramid is pleasant to see
from a distance. Close up, it is not so pleasant. There is a remarkably ugly clock tower, the streets are oppressively narrow, very
steep, and the beautiful bay just behind the town is littered with
refuse. After you have wandered for ten minutes up and down the
winding streets of Poros, you feel like a bee in a honeycomb. Poros
is a non-island, having the advantage that it can be reached in less
than an hour from Athens by hydrofoil. Item, it is easy to reach.
Item, it is fashionable. Item, it is ferociously expensive. Item, it has
no history. Then why do so many people come to the island?

"I will tell you why," said Alexander. "Not for Poros, not for the
smell of the lemon groves, but for the little bays scattered all round
the coast, for the sandy beaches and the pines coming down to the
sea. I know a little bay in Calauria, which is a peninsula connected
to Poros, where you have the illusion that nothing can possibly
happen to you except that you will spend your life sleeping and
eating and bathing. The world comes to an end. There is no history
—only the pines, the sun and the sea!"

The Lost Temple

In 322 B.C., the year after the death of Alexander the Great, the great orator Demosthenes was fleeing for his life. The order for his arrest and execution had been signed by Antipater, the friend of Aristotle. Demosthenes knew he could expect no mercy, for he had spent most of his career fighting against the Kings of Macedon for all the harm they had done to the Greek city states. He slipped out of Athens only just in time, and sailed for the island of Calauria, where he hoped to obtain sanctuary in the temple of Poseidon. The temple was inviolable ground. He seems to have known that Antipater had no respect for sanctuaries.

The man sent in search of him was Archias, a former actor, born in Italy. As Plutarch tells the story, Archias with his company of Thracian spearmen reached the temple only a few hours after Demosthenes. Archias wanted no trouble. He began to flatter Demosthenes, to soothe him, to employ his actor's voice in a wide range of endearments and subtle invitations. Demosthenes, who had seen the police captain acting out roles on the stage, remained unmoved.

"I am as little moved by your play-acting now as I was in the past," Demosthenes said, and when Archias became angry and threatening, he went on: "Ah, now you speak like the genuine Macedonian oracle. Up to this time you were merely playing a part. Now you must wait a while until I have written a few words to my family."

So for a little while longer Demosthenes remained within the inviolable sanctuary in full view of Archias and the Thracian spearmen, who were wondering whether to spear him to death on the spot or whether to remove him bodily from the temple before executing him. Demosthenes took out a scroll and prepared to write with his quill pen. It was his habit to chew on the feathers whenever he wrote or whenever he was deep in thought, and they were not particularly surprised to see him with the feathers in his mouth, but they were surprised when he lay down on the temple stones and covered his face with his gown. They thought he was trembling with fear. They shouted at him that he was effeminate and fainthearted and a coward because he had covered his face. They did not know he had sucked poison from the feathers.

Archias stepped into the temple and began to cajole him again, saying that Antipater merely wanted to make a new friend. The poison was already working. Demosthenes uncovered his face and said: "Now you may play the role of Creon in the tragedy, and throw my body to the dogs. As for me, I shall depart, O Poseidon, from thy temple alive, because I have no desire to profane it with my death, though Antipater and the Macedonians have not hesitated to defile thy sanctuary with blood." Already the hemlock was reaching down to his feet. He asked them to help him up, staggered a few yards, and fell to the ground at the foot of Poseidon's altar.

So died Demosthenes at the age of sixty-two, an old man bent and withered by his long service to Athens, on a bitter November day. It happened to be the day when the Athenian women re-enacted at the festival of the Thesmophoria the wanderings of Demeter in search of her lost daughter.

We went to Calauria to find the temple, imagining it to be on a cliff overlooking the sea, for it was impossible to imagine Poseidon inhabiting a mean place; and we thought of the temple of Athena Lindia gleaming on its headland, with columns and stairways and ceremonial courts still in place, and we expected the temple on Calauria to be equally impressive, while noting that the information in the guidebooks was meager, evasive and contradictory. One guidebook said it was in the north of the peninsula and could be reached in a forty-minute walk from the Monastery of the Panayia, another said it was in the southwest and could be reached in a little over an hour. The shopkeepers on Poros shook their heads when we asked about the temple, and it was evident that they had never seen it. Puzzled, we asked for photographs, but there were none; or postcards, but there was not a single postcard of Poros or Calauria in all the shops on the waterfront. We thought the candy-seller might know, but he only laughed. "You'll never find it," he said, and he began to twitch the arms and legs of his black monkey.

On the waterfront there were a few boats bobbing in the waves, for the straits are narrow and every passing ship throws a great wave hurtling across the straits. The boatman was a clean-limbed, handsome boy of about sixteen, who would not have looked out of place riding a horse on the Parthenon frieze. We asked about the temple. He said he would be very pleased to take us to Calauria; as for the temple, he believed it had been swallowed up in an earthquake. He had lived all his life in Poros, and never met anyone who had set eyes on it. We remonstrated. Temples do not disappear. Two Germans had written learned accounts of their excavations; every guidebook described the exact location of the temple, though in each guidebook the location differed. He said happily: "It may have fallen into the sea. Wherever it is, it is high up. I will rest in my boat while you climb." Then he pulled the string to start the motor, and the little boat went out into the straits, riding the tidal waves.

It was one of those brilliant hot days when the sky is like a blue sail and the sea is sprinkled with the white caps which the Greeks call "lambkins." The town of Poros, dreadful and somnolent, became beautiful again, and there was the scent of the lemon groves. The honeycomb of squat houses came into focus, each separate house forming an essential part of the grand design. Then the town came to an end, and at the end of the straits, before the island curved into a bay, one single white house stood low on the waterfront. It was a romantic little house, standing there at the foot of the cliffs, resembling a garden house or a pleasance, with columns decorating the single room which looked out on the open sea. So the ancient Greeks had built their houses: three walls, a roof, two or three columns. And as I wondered at the art and simplicity of the designers, the boat pulled toward the shore. It was not a pleasance but an abbatoir; the dead kids were impaled on hooks; and the smell of blood came over the sea.

Beyond the bay Calauria rose like a vast green pine cone, a vivid mountain, beautifully shaped, with only the wall of a monastery interrupting the flow of the pines. In the bay a small burned-out island with a ruined Venetian fort seemed to be floating away. The sea sparkled, and as we chugged across the bay, seeing no houses except for the white chalk-line of the monastery scrawled among the pines, there was the sense of an exquisite freshness: the island of pines was untouched: no holiday makers had ever come to desecrate the place; it was virgin still in the morning of the world.

The holiday makers, of course, had arrived long before, and they were sensibly drinking in a little café bar near the dock. It was this bay, so close to Poros and yet so distant, that Alexander had spoken about and dreamed about during long-drawn New York winters. The pines came down to the sea, the birds sang, the air was clean and succulent. It was a stiff climb to the monastery, and a stiffer climb to the top of the mountain. There was another outdoor bar near the monastery, and two black-robed monks were sunning themselves over a glass of beer, contentedly gazing out to sea. The monastery was dedicated to Our Lady, the Fountain of Life. As usual, the eighteenth century monks had chosen the site well. There is a pleasant arcaded courtyard and a small church remarkable only because it was so well lit, with blue and white walls, with no heavy parade of icons plated with silver. Outside the church an inscription read:

> *Beneath this marble*
> *Are deposited in Christ the mortal remains*
> *of*
> *Brudnell J. Bruce*
> *Late ensign of the British Foot Guards*
> *who having accompanied*
> *His Majesty's Ambassador from England*
> *Unhappily died of a fever at Poros*
> *On the eighth day of October*
> *1828*

We asked one of the women serving at the bar how to reach the temple of Poseidon. She pointed to a gap between the trees, said: "Follow the path," and began to wash out the beer bottles.

The path followed a small stream for about twenty yards and

then vanished. The stream was hidden among ferns and purple thistles, thick brambles and osiers; it glinted in the dark, a thin silvery trickle. The poet Friedrich Hölderlin had spoken of "the silver streams of Calauria slipping down to the sea, to the ancient waters of the Father," but with one foot we could have dammed the stream. And soon it vanished altogether, and even the sound of its murmuring was lost.

The whole mountain was covered with pines, most of them adorned with their little white bleeding cups, the bark sticky with the drops of resin; and we argued whether the ancient Greeks drank the resinated wine which I find detestable, while the sun pelted us, for the trees offered no shade. I calculated that there was enough resin on Calauria to sour the taste of Greek wine for generations to come. New paths would appear. Sometimes we found four or five paths branching off in as many directions; and as we climbed higher, always following the widest of the paths, the air became lighter and sweeter, while the scent of the pines grew stronger. When we turned, we would see the sandy bay and the little island with its ruined fort, or else we would see a wall of trees all oozing resin. Once we came upon some woodcutters and when we asked the direction of the temple of Poseidon, they pointed westward toward a distant peak.

"How long will it take?"

"About forty minutes," they said. "But you can't miss it—just follow the path."

But there was no path, nothing that anyone could recognize as a path. Only the boulders and the pines with their little white cups. The stream had vanished long ago.

We were sure the temple would emerge long before we came to

it, and so we marched in the direction of the peak, our faces sun-
burned, our hands sticky with resin. We came to a forester's hut,
where an old man sat brooding alone, his face so deeply lined and
scorched by the sun that it resembled an old shriveled fruit; and
when we asked him how to reach the temple, he rose slowly,
wandered into the hut and came out with a young fresh-faced
woman, who said the temple was on the saddle between the two
peaks, far below us. She had never been there, but they had always
told her it was there.

"It's in the woods," she said. "Down there, far, far down."

She was like a woman talking in a fairy tale about some un-
imaginable castle lost among misty precipices, while the sun lit the
faces of her children who gathered fearfully at her skirts.

"Few people come up here," she went on. "The children don't
see many people."

She led us along a path so that she could point out the direction
better, and at the end of the path she pointed once again to the
saddle, to the lake of blue pines below.

"I've never been there," she said, "but they say that even when
you are in the woods, you have difficulty in finding it. Just a few
stones!"

We had climbed for an hour, and were in no mood to spend
another hour searching for "a few stones." We slithered down the
mountain, and when we reached the bar near the landing stage the
barman shouted: "Did you find the temple?"

"No."

"I'm not surprised. There's only one man who knows where the
temple is. He is in Athens."

"When will he return?"

"God knows!"

We drank his beer, and he said: "People come here four or five times a year to see the temple, but unless this man goes with them they never see it."

"What is the temple like?"

"It's nothing—nothing but a few stones."

Aegina

THERE ARE EMPIRES which have left nothing of themselves behind, having vanished so completely that we scarcely know of their existence. Their great buildings have crumbled into dust, their writings have vanished, their gods and their histories are unknown. Sometimes, when flying over the deserts of Iraq and Persia, you can see the shapes of ancient cities engraved in the sand, and no one knows who lived in them, for the archaeologists have not yet got down to work, and even the shapes of these cities can be seen only briefly at dawn or at dusk, when the sun is slanting in the right direction; they survive for only a few moments each day. A hundred years ago who suspected there had been a great civilization in Crete?

So it was with Aegina, once a greater power than Athens, with a vast population, possessing slaves and treasure in abundance and a fleet which sailed all over the eastern Mediterranean. We know about its athletes, for Pindar sang of them. There was a great school of sculpture, as we know from the fifteen surviving figures of the temple of Aphaia which can now be seen in the Glyptothek in Munich and from twenty other figures scattered in twenty museums in Europe; but that is all we know. We do not know what went before, for nothing has survived of earlier sculptures, and we know that nothing came afterward, for Aegina was destroyed. It is one of the heavy lessons of antiquity that whole civilizations can be torn up from the roots, as though they had never been.

There was a time when Aegina possessed a vast banking system and sent embassies to Pharaoh. The island produced the first coins ever minted in Europe; the Aeginetan drachma stamped with the sea tortoise remained for many years the standard currency of Greece. The islanders were the best sailors in Europe, and at some unknown date before Athenian history began to be written, they inflicted a crushing naval defeat on Athens which was never forgotten. Under Pericles the Athenians took their revenge. The Aeginetans were expelled from their island and sold into slavery. The history of Aegina came to an end.

We know so little about the ancient history of Aegina that nearly all of it could be written down on a single page. The page would begin with Aeacus, the son of Zeus and grandfather of Achilles, who was believed to be the island's first ruler and lawgiver. A stern and wise judge, who once delivered Greece from the plague by the expedient of appealing to his father Zeus, he became like Minos and Rhadamanthos one of the kingly judges of the underworld. At some remote period before the Trojan War he left Argos and settled in Aegina. Then came invasions from Crete and Epidaurus, and later the Dorians conquered the island. By 700 B.C. Aegina was the ruling power in the Saronic Gulf. In its heyday, according to Aristotle, it had a slave population of 470,000. Today there are only twelve thousand people on the island. So have the mighty fallen.

Pericles called Aegina "the eyesore of Piraeus," but it was an eyesore only because it threatened the growing power of Athens. It is one of the most pleasant and beautiful of the islands, the mountains wonderfully carved, with rolling valleys and great sweeps of pine. There are vineyards, cornfields, orchards, almost no factories. The air of Athens smells of exhaust fumes, but here the air is pure. There are good roads, a rarity among the islands. From the crests of the hills there are staggering views over the blue Saronic Gulf, and the people are rosy cheeked. One can fall hopelessly in love with Rhodes and Samos, and I suspect that one could fall just as easily in love with Aegina.

Only the town of Aegina is disappointing and colorless, oddly uninviting, as though there was a blight on it. The gimcrack curio shops are not worth entering, and the narrow winding streets seem to lead nowhere. Except for the charming little blue-domed chapel of St. Nicholas in the harbor, the churches are uniformly hideous. There is nothing to see in the town except a small drab museum with a few prehistoric vases and some pale plaster casts of the great figures from the temple of Aphaia.

The museum is not a place where anyone would want to stay for any length of time; it has all the attractions of a concrete pillbox. Low roofed and ugly, with none of the charm which occasionally can be found in provincial museums—the new museum at Tinos, for example, possesses a proper monumentality even though it has very little to show—this museum seemed to survive by virtue of a prolonged act of desperation, being merely the implausible substitute for the museum which would rightfully have been here, if all the treasures of Aegina had not been rifled. Except for the columns of the temple of Aphaia, Aegina has nothing to show for its glorious past.

Still, there is the possibility that the museum may one day come into its own. According to Pausanias, there were three temples in the town, one to Apollo, one to Aphrodite, and one to Dionysus, and in honor of Aeacus there was a great marble-walled enclosure with reliefs depicting the embassies of the Greeks as they came to demand from Aeacus that he should intervene with Zeus against the plague. We know the site of the temple of Aphrodite, for a single fluted column survives along the seacoast, but the other temples have not yet been discovered. The fluted column is a sad thing, crumbling to powder. It stands there in lonely grandeur, as though surprised by its continuing existence.

The Athenians, in destroying Aegina, cannot have destroyed everything. They had no reason to destroy the temples, and it would never have occurred to them to destroy the holy places on the island. Many of them must remain below the surface of the earth. Like Crete, Aegina smells of buried treasure. Some day very soon a peasant drawing his plow across a field may find the finial of some long-forgotten temple, the excavators and archaeologists will be summoned, and a new chapter in the ancient history of Aegina will be written.

A Hill White with Churches

It was the fate of Aegina to be continually destroyed. Again and again its cities were sacked, its people carried off into captivity, its records destroyed. The island seemed to exist only to provide plunder. In the Middle Ages it became the plaything of one conqueror after another.

Some four miles inland there stands the huge grey fortresslike rock of Palaeochora crowded with white churches, with the ruins of a mediaeval castle on the summit. Thistles and wild flowers grow along the slopes, where once there was a city. In its own time it was an important city living under the protection of the Byzantine empire and possessing one of the inestimable treasures of Christendom—the head of St. George in a golden casket. Palaeochora, being out of reach of the pirates, became the capital of the island and the seat of the bishop. The people had fled from the seacoast during the time of the Saracen raids of the ninth century, and soon from the safety of their city on the hill they became pirates themselves. When the Crusaders conquered Constantinople, Aegina fell first to the Venetians and then to a succession of Frankish lords, being owned for a while by Otho de Cicon, an exemplary soldier who lent five thousand ducats to the Latin emperor, receiving as surety one of the arms of John the Baptist. It was the age when relics acquired commercial importance. The Catalans, astute merchants, took possession of the mountain and were followed once more by the Venetians, who removed the precious head of St. George to Venice where it remains to this day.

The Venetians stamped the Lion of St. Mark on the city, and made it so completely their own that even today, when the city has vanished, vestiges of their rule remain. They were hard taskmasters. When they conquered, they left no doubt who was in command. The story is told of a Venetian general who came to Palaeochora and found the local lords of the place still insisting upon the validity of their patents of nobility, their land deeds and their hereditary privileges. The general demanded that all these documents should be submitted to him. He placed them all in a sack and some time later handed the sack back to them. There was nothing left of the documents—they had been nibbled by mice. When the lords of the place threatened to emigrate en masse, the Venetian general laughed.

Venetian rule ended temporarily when the corsair Khair-ed-Din, better known as Barbarossa, landed on the coast and stormed the city in 1537. Barbarossa had no interest in gaining a capital; he wanted treasure and slaves, and these he found in abundance. Some of the Aeginetans escaped into the hills, and when Barbarossa had gone they returned to rebuild the city on its ruins. The Venetians came again in 1654, and once more the city was sacked. A few years later when a French fleet put in at the island they found no one alive. The island had become a desert.

Today no one lives on the mountain; there are only the thistles, the white churches, the crumbling pathways. There must be at least thirty churches there, though some of them are scarcely larger than cupboards. One of the largest of the churches stands at the bottom of the hill; it has recently been split in half by blasting from a neighboring quarry, but three frescoes of saints remain, protected by a few inches of roof.

Some of these churches have survived from the thirteenth century and are built in the form of a Greek cross. Most of them are open to the winds and the rain. What is astonishing is that so many frescoes survive. Tourists have scrawled their names over them, the frosts of winter have cracked the surfaces, time has peeled the paint from the walls, and still they remain. The church of St. George the Catholic, built by the Venetians, preserves a multitude of faded paintings including the portraits of David and Solomon wearing their imperial robes. Though the faces are scarred, and someone has evidently amused himself by scratching over them with a nail, they have a breathtaking splendor as they stand in a lost corner of an abandoned church, still dressed in scarlet and white, purple and gold, against a sea-green background. The church was consecrated by the Venetians, but these are not Venetian paintings, for they are wholly Byzantine and glitter like jewels.

Over the entrance of the church a long-forgotten Venetian general, Antonio Barbaro, has inscribed his name and titles and the date on which he took possession of the church:

TEMPORES YNDICATUS CLARISSIMI
DOMINI ANTONII BARBARO
DIGNISSIMI CONSILIARI
NAUPLII ROMANIE
DIE PRIM APRILIS
MCDXXXIII

It was All Fool's Day, 1433, when the proud Antonio Barbaro wrote these words in bold lettering over the church. His name could have brought little comfort to the Greeks on the island who had seen too many barbarians in their midst.

Only the yellow butterflies wander over the hill, in the echoing silence of a summer afternoon. Along the crumbling pathways one small church leads to another, each honoring a saint, each with its small altar where the spiders build their homes; and though the churches crowd together, they look lonely and desolate on those windswept heights. From the top of the hill, far away across the gulf you can see Piraeus with its stain of brown smoke floating out to sea and the snail tracks of ships shining like watered silk. The only sound comes from the faint hissing of the thistles in the wind.

The Temple of Aphaia

She is a mysterious goddess, and even in ancient times there were few who knew her origins. Some said she came from Crete and was really Dictynna, the half-sister of King Minos, who fell in love with her and pursued her until she jumped over a cliff in despair, only to fall among nets which were being left out to dry. She became the guardian goddess of the nets of fishermen. Her adventures were not yet over, for in her desire to escape from Crete she hurled herself on the first boat leaving the island, and the sailors discussed among themselves who would take possession of her. The boat was approaching Aegina when they laid violent hands on her. She jumped overboard and swam to shore, hiding from the sailors in a cave below a rocky cliff. On that cliff, they say, her temple was built.

There were others who said she was Artemis or Athena in disguise, and Pausanias maintained that she was Hecate, goddess of the underworld, with a single head, not Hecate the three-headed, the goddess who looks to the past, the present and the future. Then there were those who maintained that the name Aphaia meant the "not dark" to distinguish her from Hecate, who was "all-dark," so that instead of being Hecate she was the opposite of Hecate, being the bright sun of every day rather than the moon of the underworld. Still others said she was Britomartis, who was or was not the same as Dictynna. Perhaps she was all these, perhaps none. It is even possible that the goddess Aphaia was the principal goddess of the Aeginetans long before the Dorian invasion and her origin is therefore lost in the mists of time.

Her temple is one of the wonders of Greece, standing on the brow of a pine-clad hill overlooking the sea. Imagine the Parthenon set among woods, with the sea lapping at the foot of the Acropolis, and you have the temple of Aphaia. The power is there. In the thrust of the columns there is a divine strength and absolute authority; she is a goddess who never for an instant doubted her sovereignty, her dominion over the island. It is not necessary to know who she was; it is enough that she is there, superbly in command.

There are only a few temples in Greece where you have the feeling that an abundant life still flows among the columns. Life flows round the Parthenon, but there is no life in the temple of Hephaestus overlooking the agora in Athens, though it is the most splendidly preserved of all Greek temples. Life swirls and eddies around the golden gateway of the temple of Apollo at Naxos, and it is abundantly present on the heights of Lindos. In Delphi and Delos it is not to be found in the crumbled stones, but in the landscape. In Mycenae, too, you can recognize the presence of an ancient mystery still quivering with vitality, though the kings of Mycenae have been dead for three thousand years.

Perhaps it is because the temple of Aphaia looks so fresh and new, with twenty columns still standing, that it acquires the appearance of a temple still in use, or perhaps it is because the gentle swelling of the columns suggests a springing life within them. Most of the architraves are in place. The massive stone platform is hardly damaged. Two columns of the prodomos are still standing erect with their capitals in place. The Doric columns, each with their twenty flutings, stand squarely on the stone platform. An imperious vigor rises from the stone floor.

What is strange is that the temple of Aphaia left so little record in history. Pausanias mentions it briefly, adding that Pindar composed a song about the goddess for the Aeginetans, but only two lines of the song have survived and they tell us nothing about her. He wrote many odes in honor of Aeginetan athletes, summoning the gods to witness the prowess of the young heroes, but never appealing to Aphaia. Where we expect to find her, she has vanished.

For years scholars thought the temple was erected to Athena. Charles Cockerell, the young English architect who found the pedimental statues in 1810, assumed as a matter of course that the archaic goddess who stood in the center of the west pediment, helmeted and bearing a heavy ornamental shield, was Athena in all her majesty. Who else could it be? She had the look of a powerful goddess presiding over battles, fearless and virginal. At her feet warriors were engaged in mortal combat, and it was assumed that they were the sons of Aeacus at war with the Trojans, and it was known that Athena had favored them. Then, not far from the temple, some inscriptions were found reading: "Boundary of the enclosure consecrated to Athena." The case was proved. Aphaia vanished again, and Athena reigned supreme. Then in 1901 Adolf

Furtwängler, the German archaeologist who was to die a few years later of fever contracted in Aegina, found in the foundations of the temple a broken slab inscribed in archaic lettering with the names of Aphaia and of the priest who officiated at the first ceremonies:

Though a small part of the slab on the left was broken off, the inscription could be easily read: "While Kleoitas was priest, the temple of Aphaia rose from its foundations, the altar and gold and ivory statue were erected, and the enclosure was surrounded by walls." The broken slab stands at the left of the door of the poverty-stricken museum in Aegina. It is the most precious of all the museum's possessions, for it celebrates in our century the rebirth of a beautiful and once powerful goddess.

She stands in the Glyptothek in Munich as though all the power in the world were concentrated in her hands, more imperious than any other goddess carved by the Greeks. She has a full face and a rich crown of thickly waved hair, and a half-smile curves her lips. Her gown falls in intricate folds, once painted scarlet and gold, her feet are bare, one hand hovers in the air; the spear is missing, and so she appears to be stretching out her hand in welcome. In this way the accidents of time improve on sculpture.

Of the gold and ivory statue nothing remains, but it cannot have been very different from this statue of her. It stood within the cella

and like the statue of Athena in the Parthenon must have reached
to the roof. To her the Aeginetans brought their offerings, including
the prows of the Samian ships they conquered in battle. These
prows were shaped like boars' heads, and since the whole of the
Samian fleet was destroyed, the prows too must have reached close
to the roof. She was a warrior goddess, and the boars must have
pleased her.

There were earlier temples on this spot, but the present temple
may very well date from the time of the victory over Samos. Aegina
was then at the height of her power, in alliance with Crete and
Egypt, with the most powerful fleet in the eastern Mediterranean.
She was the mistress of the sea, proud and careless. Less than a
century later the Athenians reduced her to impotence, and then at
last the temple of Aphaia became the temple of Athena.

The Other Island

LIKE AEGINA the islands died, and sometimes they came to life again. Rhodes died, and came to life under the Knights of St. John and died again under the Turks. Patmos and Cos sleep their long sleep, and Myconos, which never lived, dies every day under the weight of the tourists who come to that barren island to escape out of history altogether. Chios died its many deaths, though the shipowners grew fat with trade, and Samos perished altogether when the Greeks fled to avoid the exactions of the Turks. A wave hurled from the island of Santorin destroyed the Minoan empire, but soon the Cretans were manning their pirate ships again. The history of the Greek islands is one of continual death and perpetual resurrection.

These islands, then, have a habit of dying and being reborn: a habit which is eminently suitable to the Islands of the Blessed. Take, for example, the island of Syra, which played no part in ancient history and produced only one person of eminence, the philosopher Pherecydas, said to have been the teacher of Pythagoras. The works of Pherecydas are lost, and all that is known about him is that he lived in a cave in the north of the island. But we know the island well from the pages of Homer. For him it was the most desirable of islands, precisely because it was outside history. Eumaius, the swineherd, came from Syra, and he enjoyed describing his island to Odysseus:

> *There is an island called Syra—you may know the name,*
> *Over beyond Delos, where the sun turns in its course,*
> *With not too many people, and a rich soil*
> *Teeming with sheep and cattle, corn and wine.*
> *And there is no famine there, and no sickness*
> *Ever strikes the people; when they grow old,*
> *The gods appear to them—Artemis comes, and Apollo,*
> *The Lord of the Silver Bow, strikes them with his gentle arrows,*
> *And gently they die.*

Eumaius has a story to tell of how the peaceful island was raided by Phoenician pirates, and how he himself as a child was spirited away in the company of his nurse, a Phoenician slave, and sold in the market place of Ithaca. Yet Apollo protected him, for he was dealt with kindly. In that small island his father had been king; now he was a swineherd, remembering the vanished glory; and what he remembered chiefly was that men grew old gracefully and there were no wars.

Eumaius described Syra as all the other islanders would have liked to describe their islands; prosperous, fertile, and peaceful, with not too many people. Today Syra is prosperous again, and there are not too many people, but it is almost beyond belief that it was ever fertile. It owes its prosperity to the accidents of trade, having become a coaling port in the nineteenth century. The merchants of Syra knew how to build; and of all the islands of the Aegean it is the only one with any pretensions to architecture. There are streets which might be in Paris; there is even an opera house. Yet the city lives on its past, for the coal ships are almost extinct, and today its chief wealth derives from the export of loukoumi, which the world knows as Turkish delight. All round the harbor are shops advertising loukoumi so insistently that you might think that appetite would be dulled by repetition.

Syra is not in the least like the Greek islands of the travel posters. There are no ruins, no ancient battlements. It has about it no other romance than the romance of ordinary people living out their ordinary lives. Yet after the long loneliness of the islands, Syra comes as a welcome relief. Rhodes preserves the courtliness of the Knights, Samos is Turkish still, Heracleion wears a perpetual provincial air, and Thasos is no more than a village surrounding an ancient agora. Syra, being the capital of the Cyclades, regards itself with a lordly air, very pleased with its restaurants, cafés and bars, and most of all pleased because it has miraculously survived the fate reserved for the islands: it is not a museum. No one knows where Eumaius lived, and no one cares. They will point to a cave somewhere in the north of the island and say that Pherecydas lived there, and quickly pass on to more important matters.

What the Syriots enjoy more than anything else is parading up and down the streets—it is an enjoyment they share with the ancient Greeks. The Athenians have no parade ground. Syra has two.

One is the harbor esplanade, the other is Miaoulis Square only a street length away. Here after the day's work they take the air, wheel their prams, show off their wives, discuss the weather, and disport themselves with quiet elation; and that interminable care-free voyage brings color to their cheeks and appetite to their stomachs. There is nothing heroic about them. They are in love with life and movement and talk, and see no reason for more daring adventures. In much the same way Socrates and Plato paraded along their colonnades, finding in conversation adventures enough for a lifetime.

So many battles were fought in the islands that the mind reels; they were a forcing ground for heroes, forever storming the parapets. Every island had its nest of pirates. Anarchy ruled, as one little princeling after another granted himself dazzling titles, enslaved the people, and taught them to bear arms against the neighboring islands. In the north of Lesbos there stands the ruined castle of Methymna, a gaunt and savage place with walls ten feet thick high on a promontory overlooking the hills of Troy. The fortress was built by the Genoese family of the Gateluzi, which had intermarried with obscure princesses of the Byzantine court. For more than a century they governed the island, until they were themselves enslaved by the Turks and compelled to pay tribute to the sultan, who wearied of them and finally tossed them out of the island as though they were a handful of pebbles thrown into the sea.

Yet how well the Gateluzis built their castle! How magnificently they carved out of the living rock those huge and towering battlements! The fortress is a heap of wild ruins inhabited by chattering crows. But it is not for the absurd Genoese princelings that one remembers Methymna. One remembers it because the village which winds at the foot of the mountain is quietly beautiful, and because Arion, the inventor of dithyrambic poetry, was born there, and because the head of Orpheus was washed up on those shores after his body had been dismembered by the Thracian women, and because Daphnis and Chloe frolicked on those shores. The ancient legends have outlived the Gateluzis, who are no more than footnotes to footnotes of mediaeval history; the head of Orpheus still bleeds, the voices of Daphnis and Chloe are still heard.

The islands created enduring legends: not the legends of warriors and princelings, but of lovers and wanderers and visionaries. From a cave in Patmos St. John saw the ends of the earth and the end of the worlds. From a throne on Chios Homer sang of disastrous wars and joyful wanderings. In the market place of Samos, among the fountains of blue air, Pythagoras mapped out the laws of mathematics and music, and Theodoros mapped out the laws of architecture. Homer, Sappho, Arion and Aristarchus were all islanders; and western poetry has its origins in the islands off the coast of Asia Minor. All that is good and fresh and virile came from those islands, where the lucid air taught men lucidity. The islands were places of refuge, where the mind could rise free.

Almost the islands escape from the map; they are climates of the heart, places where the soul wanders. Like our mysterious island of Ktio, they are almost without substance. Marble becomes light, the sea becomes a dimension of the heavens, and the happy wanderer finds himself soaring through spaces of sunlit air as though there was nothing so heavy as earth to impede his progress. Apollo reigns; all is quietness; and soon another island appears on the blue horizon.

Index